# IDEAL ME

**Discovering your call in a cluttered world**

## Definition of CALL:

**A summons to a particular course of action, influenced by the divine.**

# IDEAL ME

### Discovering your call in a cluttered world

## GLEN ALEXANDER GUYTON

A CULTURAL GUIDEBOOK
FOR YOUTH, YOUNG ADULTS
AND THOSE WHO SUPPORT THEM

IDEAL ME

Copyright © 2018 by Glen Guyton

GuyStar Enterprises LLC
3103 Highline Trl
San Antonio, TX 78261
www.IDEALmeBook.com
Book and Cover Design: Ron Tinsley, www.prophetiksoul.com
Editor: June Galle Krehbiel
WebDesign: Sushe Design, www.sushedesign.com

ISBN: 978-0-692-14275-2
Library of Congress Control Number: 2018907620

Ordering Information:
Quantity sales. Special discounts are available on quantity purchases by religious groups, associations, schools, and others for use in training, professional development, or as conference materials. For details, contact BOOK SALES at the address above.

ATTENTION: ASSOCIATIONS, SCHOOLS, ORGANIZATIONS and RELIGIOUS GROUPS:

For more information on workshops; to book keynotes or learn more about leadership development for youth and young adults, please visit www.GlenGuyton.com.

Printed in the United States of America

First Edition

14 13 12 11 10 / 10 9 8 7 6 5 4 3 2 1

# Acknowledgements

To my wife, Cyndi, thanks for listening to my stories over and over again. Thank you for sticking by my side as I figured myself out. May all your dreams come true.

To my wonderful children, Andre-A and Alex, you were the test case for a lot of the information contained in this book. Thanks for helping to shape who I am. This book is really for the two of you. Believe in your gifts.

To my mother, thank you for sharing your faith with me. There was no greater gift that you could have given me.

To Bishop L.W. Francisco III, thank for being a father to me and for picking up where my father left off. I could not have picked a better mentor.

To my C3 family and former youth in Hampton, Virginia, thanks to each and every one of you whoever called me "MinGlen." You all wrote this book for me, you gave me the opportunity to live out my calling, and you will always be in my heart.

To my sensei, thanks for helping me wake up and execute my call. You are a blessing and an inspiration.

Most of all, I thank God for the inspiration and the experiences that helped me write this book. God is greater than I am, and I am grateful for the opportunity to give back and share my blessings with others.

# Table of Contents

# Preface

No book, no author can change your life. No magic formula or fairy dust will appear to make that happen. Only you can do that. This book is not for everyone, but it may be for you. Welcome to the adventure of discovering your IDEAL me. Following your divine call will not guarantee happiness, but that call to your IDEAL life is like a song that you can't get out of your head. Once the call has been heard, there is no satisfaction for those who choose not to answer.

This book is a curated collection of my thoughts and experiences. I have worked with young people from a variety of backgrounds. After spending more than half my life leading people in my roles as an Air Force officer, business person, teacher, pastor, and father, I have picked up a little wisdom here and there. I have seen people fail miserably and succeed greatly. I have mentored hundreds of students and young adults.

So how should you read this book? The best way is to pick one or two pieces of information and take action. Skim it, scan it, or read it word for word; it doesn't really matter. Sure, I think everything I wrote here is important, but it may not be important for you. As you read, from time to time lay the book aside; then immediately apply what you have learned. After a period of time, come back, pick up one or two pieces of information relevant to your journey; then apply those. Repeat as needed. Life is a series of ups and downs. We go through different phases of need as we mature or as our circumstances change. Pick whatever chapter or guidance that you need at the time. There are no rules to reading this book, just like there are not set rules defining what your version of the IDEAL life is. This book is just one tool to help you improve your life. Ultimately, you will be the champion of your own success and I am happy to be along for the ride.

—Glen Guyton

# Introduction

What is the IDEAL me? This book's purpose is not to tell you who you should be. It is not to help you become more like me or more like some iconic figure that is the epitome of success in popular culture. What we do proves who we are, even in how we express our giftedness. The things we do and choose in life reflect who we are, not the other way around. What we choose and what we do doesn't shape us; on the contrary we are a reflection of our choices. Our actions are the fruit we bear. With this book you will learn how to discover and cultivate your gifts in such a way that you don't betray who you truly are. You betray your gifts by not producing or by producing far below your potential.

If you are seeking to be the next Bill Gates, the next Stephen Curry, or the next Gigi Hadid, this book is not for you. You are not them and you are probably not equipped to live their lives. We often envy the lives of other people and deep inside we wish that we could be them. We are drawn to the posts of family and friends and covet their exciting lives. Yet, we see them only at a single moment in time. We want to be fabulous like the Instagram and reality TV stars, yet we fail to realize their lives are well-scripted. They have personal designers and professional marketers helping them to look perfect when they step into the public eye. We have no clue what it took for them to become the persons that they are, the personas we see.

Sometimes we can be fooled. For many years Bill Cosby was an iconic figure in the African-American community because of his clean comedy and because of the all-American father character he played on television. Well, that image of Bill Cosby has been shattered by multiple allegations of sexual assault: the true man behind the mask has allegedly been revealed to be quite different from that of Dr. Heathcliff Huxtable, Cosby's TV character. Each week the paparazzi and TMZ expose the flaws of our reality TV stars and media darlings, and we see that they are not as perfect as we had imagined them to be.

Much of our identity is related to what we do in life. For many of us this means our chosen career, but this is not always the case. (We will discuss that later in the book as we examine "calling" in chapter five.) Our calling can be quite distinct from where we work or how we make a living. Some of us find work to simply be a means to an end, a necessary inconvenience that funds our true passions. Others, like me, have been blessed to have job and calling linked closely together. My calling, in fact, has paid the bills. I left the military to pursue ministry, a higher calling for me. I took a $20,000 a year pay cut and I haven't looked back. Yes, maybe I missed out on that military retirement check, but I gained so much more.

Do you ever discover yourself in situations where you feel like you don't belong? I am often the only person of color in many settings where I live and work. This is mainly because of the choices that my parents and I made when I was growing up. This is not to say that black or brown people are not educated or can't achieve. Rather, the communities where we live often direct us into certain paradigms. Public schools are zoned by neighborhoods, so they are often economically and racially segregated. I chose schools and programs that fit my educational goals. I was not satisfied going to the school in the suburban working-class neighborhood where we lived. I took a risk to leave my friends and ride an hour and a half on the bus to other schools. I also chose to go to a Presbyterian Church camp while nearly all of my friends were Baptist or Catholic. Sometimes it felt like I was the weird one in my neighborhood.

Plus, I was interested in things many of my friends weren't. I was a nerd, a bookworm, but I still enjoyed sports, BMX bikes, and rough-housing with the fellas. Yet, when I ventured outside my assigned school zone, in many situations I was the only black kid. I decided that if everyone were going to know me, then they were going to know me for more than just being the black kid. I was going to be the funny kid. I was going to be the smart kid. I was going to be the kid with a ton of ideas, so that is what I became. It was my first step towards becoming "me," and finding my IDEAL healthy identity. At the time, I did not even realize it.

We have to become comfortable being the best "me" we can be. My IDEAL is not your IDEAL and I am okay with that. Sure, being Bill Gates has certain perks that I may never have. Funny as it may seem, there are certain perks to being Glen that Bill Gates may never experience. Just think—I get to take Uber to the airport and he is forced to fly in his private jet. I have an anonymity and freedom that one of the world's most famous billionaires can never recapture. Okay, maybe I would trade my Uber ride for a G6 private jet, but I cannot spend my life measuring my gifts and life against those of others. It's just not productive.

I remember watching the 2016 Rio Olympics with my family as the great Olympic swimmer Michael Phelps competed in a finals event against a Brazilian swimmer, Marcelo Chierighini. That's a name that you probably don't even remember. Chierighini was expected to challenge Phelps for the gold, but throughout warm-ups and even during the race, Chierghini was more focused on Phelps than on winning his race. Repeated camera shots showed the Brazilian staring constantly at Phelps. Not only did Chierighini not win, the Brazilian failed to medal. He turned his head several times during the 200-meter butterfly to see what Phelps was doing. Phelps, on the other hand, remained focused on being the first to touch the wall, and he did.

While we can't be blind to the world around us, we can't swim someone else's race or live out someone else's dream. It may cost us more that we could ever hope to gain.

To reach my goals, I have had to learn how to wade through all of my life experiences, all of the bits and pieces of wisdom that I have been given, and figure out the best path for my life.

The path to your IDEAL life involves answering five questions:

✓ Who am I?
✓ Where do I want to go in life?
✓ How do I stay relevant in an ever-changing world?
✓ How can I stay sharp and honed in on my IDEAL path?
✓ How do I release the baggage of my past and continue to move forward in life?

Using those five questions, I have developed the IDEAL framework for helping people just like you to discover your calling in life. Determining your call will help you develop your healthy identity in our cluttered and dynamic world.

1. **I** A M
2. I **D** E C I D E
3. I **E** V O L V E
4. I **A** D V A N C E
5. I **L** E T   G O

**I AM.** Finding your "I AM" can be a powerful, yet humbling journey. You will feel so at peace when you finally come to grips with who you are and you can comfortably share that with the world. It seems pretty simple at first glance but many people—both young and old—wrestle with that "Who am I?" question. The pressure starts as soon as you graduate from high school. Person after person asks you, "What are your plans?" The truth is few of us, even at 40 years of age, can say with confidence, "This is what I am going to do with the rest of my life"—and many fewer of us have it all figured out at the ages of 17 or 18. For many teens and young adults, you find it hard to determine what you are going to do two weeks from now, but people want you to have a 20-year career plan and a solid retirement plan the moment the principal hands you a diploma.

**I DECIDE.** Knowing and doing are two separate acts. Even if you have a good grasp of your gifts, are you putting in the necessary work to pursue your dreams? Will you be able to overcome whatever obstacles keep you from deciding to follow your IDEAL path? To be honest, some people choose not to live their IDEAL lives. They choose the easy path. They choose the path that gets them the most money or the most prestige. The IDEAL process is not about fame, fortune, or convenience. It is about deciding to maximize the gifts and talents you have been given and living a life with very few regrets. Our life is about the choices we make and no self-help book or process is going to get you to any place, except for the place that you choose to go. Your determination, your hard work, and a little wisdom will carry you far in life. You have to decide.

**I EVOLVE.** One constant in life is change. The IDEAL life is not about stagnation. We need to recognize that situations and circumstances as well as we ourselves change over time. It would be foolish for me to say that the IDEAL life you are living now will be the same one you should be living 15 years from now. Just as the jobs you have may change over time, so does our call. Evolving is also about managing expectations. As we grow and mature, our expectations change—as well as our capacity to fulfill the expectations that both we and the outside world place upon us. How we take on the world today may not be how we face it tomorrow. The decisions you make today will affect your future. So will the decisions you make tomorrow. Life changes and you must grow/change along with it.

**I ADVANCE.** While evolving is more about us changing over time and adapting to new situations, advancement is about staying sharp along the way. Even the best knife gets dull (with repeated use). Good chefs will not only regularly sharpen their knives, but they use a steel to hone that edge each time the knife is used. The honing steel makes the sharpened edge of the knife true. A knife that is honed consistently, needs to be sharpened less often. As we live out our IDEAL lives, we should constantly and consistently seek out knowledge and people that will keep us sharp. If we don't, we can get stuck and become unfulfilled.

**I LET GO.** The last part of living out our IDEAL lives is letting go of our negative past. A wise friend once told me, "Don't cling to a mistake just because you spent a lot of time making it. Release it and move forward."

Past baggage can be the most significant obstacle to stepping into the life we are created to live. Unfortunately, some of the baggage and hurt we carry was imposed on us by outside forces. The inflicted hurt, damage, and pain were beyond our control, but it is our responsibility to examine the baggage we carry and seek out healthy responses to the pain of our past. Not to oversimply this journey that we call life, but I believe that most of us can regulate how much we let those negative things affect our future. After reading this book and going through the exercises, I hope that you will leave everything negative from your past outside the door, buried away. Carry with you into the future only what you are called to be.

That IDEAL life is typically just at our fingertips, just one choice or decision away. But we can get distracted by the shiny lives of others, the overload of information, and the constant input from those around us.

Again, we have to realize that what is the IDEAL for someone else may not be our IDEAL. Many well-meaning people will tell us what they think we should do, what they would do, and what works for them. The advice they give might be very good and has actually worked for them. The advice may be sound and solid advice, but it may not be the advice that will lead you to the place you need to go.

We are given our own lives to live. We have our own set of gifts. We have our own set of talents. The way we interpret and touch the world is unique to who we are. It is our IDEAL.

## Glen's Guidance

- Go after your "I AM" even if it is a powerfully, humbling journey.
- Be determined. Work hard. Carry wisdom with you as you decide.
- Change and grow as you journey through life.
- Keep your edge sharp.
- Don't cling too tightly to the past.
- Don't get distracted. The IDEAL life is at your fingertips, just one choice or one decision away.

## Part 1

# I AM...

...the sum total of my choices, my experiences, and my environment.

# Chapter 1

## The ENVY Me

*Queen: Slave in the magic mirror, come from the farthest space,*
*through wind and darkness I summon thee. Speak! Let me see thy face.*
*Magic Mirror: What wouldst thou know, my Queen?*
*Queen: Magic Mirror on the wall, who is the fairest one of all?*
*Magic Mirror: Famed is thy beauty, Majesty. But hold, a lovely maid I see.*
*Rags cannot hide her gentle grace. Alas, she is more fair than thee.*
*—Grimm Brothers, "Snow White and the Seven Dwarfs"[3]*

Before we go any further, you need to learn my golden rule and apply it to every lesson and example that you read in this book. Glen's Golden Rule is:

# My IDEAL is not your IDEAL.

That is the most significant piece of information that a person can ever take to heart when beginning the journey of life.

> *Pay careful attention to your own work, for then you will get the satisfaction of a job well done, and you won't need to compare yourself to anyone else, for we are each responsible for our own conduct. —Galatians 6:4-5 NLT*

To be successful, you have to accept both your *gifts* and, contrary to popular belief, your *limitations* (more on that later). All of us at some point may ask ourselves questions like: *Who am I? Why was I created? What am I called to do?* Maybe you have asked yourself these questions more than once. I know I have. Our minds and our lives are cluttered with ideas, images, and possessions that distract us and constantly divide our attention.

In preparation for writing this book, I looked at a bunch of similar books. I looked at books written by famous gurus, top speakers, and various doctors. I talked to my former bosses who had written books. One has a PhD and has written a number of research and historical fiction books. His books have hundreds of pages and he seems to spit out a book every couple of years. Here I was trying to finish just one book. Even a couple of my former students were pumping out books. I was ready to trash this book and give up on the dream of being an author. Why? Because I could not write like they wrote. I was comparing my gifts to their gifts. I was a tad jealous. I was a tad envious. Those two emotions combined are always a recipe for disaster manifesting themselves in the forms of inaction and self-defeat. So I decided to stop focusing on what everyone else was doing and proceeded to hammer out this book, line by line in a way that fit *my* gifts.

With the internet and social media, we have a wealth of information at our fingertips. We can be overwhelmed with global options and a universe of fantastic possibilities, so we begin to ask those "Who am I?" questions while comparing ourselves to the media darlings we watch on television or on our connected devices. Through the World Wide Web, smart devices and various social media platforms, we can get information and connect with just about anyone in the world in an instant. Every waking minute of the day we feel compelled to check our text messages, emails, and social media accounts to see what is happening in the lives of our friends, neighbors, and even strangers. Even presidents and other people in power are known for their Twitter and social media posts.

> I believe we fail to focus on our dreams and our life goals because we are too busy online, glaring at cat pictures or checking to see which megastars are divorcing each other.

According to dscout, a web and mobile service company that helps its clients engage audiences, "*The heaviest smartphone users click, tap or swipe on their phones 5,427 times a day.* That's the top 10 percent of phone users, so one would expect it to be excessive. However, the rest of us still touch the addictive things 2,617 times a day on average. That is no small number."[4] Often this comes at the cost of us ignoring the real, live, breathing people in close proximity to us who are trying to communicate with us. We can become distant from our family, friends, and classmates even when we are sitting in the same room. During our family gatherings I try to get my teenage nieces and nephews off the phones and engaged in family games, sometimes without much success. While everyone else is laughing and talking, too often the teens are isolated in the corner with headphones and glassy eyes. That is not the way to foster relationships with the extended family.

A study by Common Sense Media says, "Half of all teens admit they are addicted to their smartphones and other mobile devices, and nearly 60 percent of parents say they think their teens are too tech-addled."[5] Why is it so difficult for many of us to discover our true calling in life? I believe we fail to focus on our dreams and our life goals because we are too busy online, glaring at cat pictures or checking to see which megastars are divorcing each other.

We give in to the clutter. We begin to think that unless we are on a reality show, our lives are without meaning. We measure our lives by followers, likes, and hits. These false measures are unrealistic and unobtainable for the vast majority of us. Yet, we keep consuming these media-driven standards of success, confusing "idol-istic" lives with idealistic lives. Living in the information age, we have become victims of information overload. It is like we have our own little magic mirrors and we constantly are seeking information about who is the fairest of them all. This massive mountain of information leads to envy and even a sense of hopelessness. We either resent the accomplishments of others or feel we cannot measure up.

Karol Markowicz wrote in her New York Post opinion piece, "There's nothing new about jealousy and envy. … What's new is our cultural acceptance of it."[6] In a world where we talk about inequality as the greatest problem we face, keeping up with the Joneses becomes a way of life. We enable the sickness of consumerism, overextending ourselves to acquire as much stuff as our friends and neighbors.

No one posts when they are sitting at home staring at the walls or in the midst of an emotional tragedy.

Do we post our true doubts and fears online? No, we post and boast about happy times. We take 20 selfies to get the one perfect "natural" shot. Sometimes I take a break from social media when I notice what some call "the envy effect" creeping into my sphere of emotion. I see my professional speaker friends traveling all over the world. I see pictures of my younger friends having babies. I read the posts of married friends who seem to love ever single moment with their spouse and a catch myself not being happy for them. I sometimes say to myself, "Why are they so lucky? How can they afford all of that?" We see the social media posts of our friends and wonder why our lives aren't filled with exotic trips, gourmet meals, and excitement 24/7. We overlook that most folks post only the best of what is going on in their lives.

But then, like many of you, when I go on a trip with my family, I post a flurry of happy pictures and cute comments. I'm that guy posting pictures of every meal and showing the great places I am touring. But you know what I am leave out? I am leaving out the part when my daughter got sick or we had to cut out some experiences to stay within budget. I leave out the photos when we are hot, tired, and sweaty. I leave out the part when we are in line, waiting for the fun to happen. No, I post only the four fun hours of my vacation day and I leave out the other 20 hours when we are doing nothing. My son rarely lets me posts pics of him. I get a lot of back-of-the-head shots. So when I ultimately get a picture of his face, it is usually after hours of negotiation. Social media creates this snapshot of perpetual joy and happiness that is reality for exactly zero percent of the human population.

The funny thing is that the only time I get hit with the envy effect is when I am bored out of my mind. When I am busy on a project or sharing real life experiences with the people I love, I am not even checking social media that much. Social media gets checked during the routine, uneventful periods of my life, like when I sit at the mechanic waiting on my car. When I am speaking in front of 3,000 people or cooking barbecue on my deck, looking at someone else's social media feed is the last thing on my mind. The online forum does not share the totality of who we are; it just shares a sliver of our lives—the part of ourselves that we *want* the world to see. Instead of wishing that our lives could be some clone of our friends' lives, we need to discover who we are called to be. We have to figure out our IDEAL life.

The IDEAL life is a journey through life that involves reflecting on those five very important questions I mentioned in the introduction. Consider these as you learn to accept your strengths and limitations:

✓ Who am I?
✓ Where do I want to go in life?
✓ How do I stay relevant in an ever-changing world?
✓ How can I stay sharp and honed in on my IDEAL path?
✓ How do I release the baggage of my past and continue to move forward in life?

Hopefully you have gotten the picture, that most of us will never be the next famous idol, Instagram model, Top Chef or sports MVP. Each and every one of us has a gift. Some gifts may be more visible than others, but we all have something to share with the world. We need to develop a realistic understanding of our life's call. We have to acquire the tools necessary to wade through the false images we consume daily. Such images will lead only to the development of a false sense of self. They will clutter our lives.

Many of us take these false images and create a mask. The mask protects us from pain—pain that we felt when we were young or when we felt too weak, inadequate, or overwhelmed to function as our authentic selves. But this pain may lead us to construct an inauthentic version of ourselves, making us only *appear* to be better, stronger, and more able to cope with the world around us.

Instead of trying to measure up to the lies in print and social media, we need to become the best versions of ourselves that we can possibly be. Instead of envying others or feeling inadequate, we must find our IDEAL "me" and ignore the clutter and noise that surrounds us daily. We have to understand how to answer our life's call. We have to understand, after careful discernment, how to grab onto something positive, some cause we truly believe in, and commit to it. "Who you are" involves finding something: a cause or a reason to exist *that is greater than yourself*. Here is a formula for you to remember:

**My IDEAL Life > My Selfish Ambition**

*If we don't understand our life's purpose when answering that divine call and if we lose our sense of self, we wind up like the walking dead (pun intended).* We are in a zombie-like state of being, wandering aimlessly, no destination in mind, and no vision. Maybe zombies eat brains because they have no minds of their own. They have no hopes, no dreams so they feed off what others have to offer. When we don't have a sense of self, like those zombies, we just move in the direction that someone else points us. That someone else might be on social media, the regular media, or some random person we hook up with at a party. We wander and wander and we do this until we eventually die—experiencing both a metaphorical and literal death. Then we just quit, we give up.

My older half-brother, Brian, was a very gifted electrician and carpenter. He was an absolute genius with his hands and people really loved him, but he had this void in his life that nothing could ever fill. He walked away from a successful career with an oil company and eventually became a drugged-out zombie. Alcohol was his poison of choice. For years he wandered around without purpose—in and out of our lives and in and out of rehab. He lived on and off the streets until eventually his wanderings took him to the bottom of a river. My brother was never able to figure out how to cope with the ups and downs of life. Although the bottle and the river eventually claimed his physical life, my brother died over and over again each time the challenges of life came upon him. He was not able to live into the rich calling of life. The demon of alcohol and past hurts cluttered his mind.

For many of you reading this book, retirement is a long way off. You may not have even taken your first job yet, but consider this: studies suggest that people who retire early have an increased risk of death as opposed to people who retire later in life.[6] Why is that? I suppose some early retirees think they have no reason to get up in the morning, which is sad. They fail to adapt to the next phase of their life. Maybe they confused their occupation with their calling. This is not just a cautionary tale for senior citizens, but for teens and young adults as well. Whether we are young or old, we must understand the gifts we possess and how we contribute to this world. If we don't understand our calling, our very existence is at risk.

We all need to learn how to cope with this gift of life we have been given. This is not to discount mental illness and significant traumatic life experiences. I am not a psychiatrist and this book does not address serious psychological or medical conditions, but, according to Natasha Tracy in the website Healthy Place, "Most teens who have been interviewed after a suicide attempt say that what causes teen suicide are feelings of hopelessness and helplessness. Suicidal teens often feel like they are in situations that have no solutions. The teens can see no way out but death. The teens feel like they have no control to change their situations."[7] *Suicidal people are not able to see how their gifts fit into this world, why they are valuable, why they too have to answer their divine call.*

It is important for teens and adults contemplating suicide to talk to a professional to determine what type of support they need to live life here. I say this with caution, but I know from experience—we can control how we react to the challenges and waves of life. Knowing where to get help and understanding that you are in trouble is a positive step in taking control of your life. We all need help from time to time. The amazing thing is that through asking for help you are not only reclaiming your own healthy self-control, but you are giving someone else the opportunity to use their gifts in service to you.

I want you to find and live your IDEAL life. But more than that, I want you to *love the life you live.*

*Heartbreak Ridge* is a movie from 1986 about Gunny Highway, an old Marine gunnery sergeant portrayed by Clint Eastwood, on his last tour of duty trying to whip a bunch of young, misfit, undisciplined recruits into shape. Eastwood's character ultimately guides the slacking soldiers to become heroes. "Improvise. Adapt. Overcome," Highway orders as he teaches them to handle everything life throws their way.

As we go through the seasons of our lives, we need to improvise (to), adapt (to), and overcome the challenges that encompass life. We have to figure out what it means to be ourselves. We have to learn how to sort through all the information and clutter to understand what it means to be our best selves.

At the same time, we have to understand our strengths and weaknesses. I know that I am not Michael Jordan, Michael Phelps, or Michael Bublé. I can't be them. I am not equipped emotionally, physically, or genetically to live the lives these gentlemen lived. I also have to be aware of my passions and what really motivates me.

Deep down I believe we all have a sense of God's call for us, but time and circumstance corrupt the creation that we are. Even with a wealth of information at our fingertips, we often cannot discern our own gifts and passions—we are too consumed with what everyone else is doing. As we receive more and more information from others about who they think we are, we pay less and less attention to who we think we are. We discount our gifts because we envy others. We have to pay attention to our IDEAL path. Attention is the psychological tool we use to tune out irrelevant information (clutter) so we can focus on what is important to us or what gifts we naturally have.

Through the processes outlined in this book, you will learn valuable tools to help you stop paying attention to everyone and everything else. You will get a framework for how to stop ignoring your personal dreams and how to stop being envious of other people. Why? Because the "me" inside of you is definitely worth paying attention to.

**Glen's Guidance**

- Seek your life's purpose or you will wind up in a zombie-like state of being.
- Focus on your dreams; stop wasting time simply wishing and watching others achieve theirs.
- Get rid of the envy business; become the best version of yourself that you can possibly be.
- Love the life you live.
- Improvise. Adapt. Overcome.

## NOTES

_____

_____

_____

_____

_____

_____

_____

_____

_____

# Chapter 2

# The Hidden Me

*I'm starting with the man in the mirror*
*I'm asking him to change his ways*
*And no message could have been any clearer*
*If you wanna make the world a better place*
*Take a look at yourself, and then make a change.*
—Michael Jackson's "Man in the Mirror"[9]

Famed performer Michael Jackson once sang a song called, "Man in the Mirror." It was all about making changes. The clear message was that if you wanted to change the world, you first had to change the person looking back at you in the mirror every morning. We all wear some sort of mask to hide our true selves. To some degree, we are all keenly aware of our differences, especially after adolescence. Prior to adolescence, we have a limited capacity for abstract reasoning; our thinking is oriented in the here and now.

According to one study, "The process of developing self-esteem is life-long and a key role in it is played by interpersonal relationships. It begins in early childhood, where a secure attachment to parents forms a basis for a healthy self-esteem, but continues in adolescence, first to include peer relations, and in adulthood to comprise the interpersonal relationships of our different social contexts and roles."[10]

As children, we are just who we are, and then one day we wake up and look in the mirror on the wall and see judgment looking back at us and we don our masks. As one researcher writes, kids don't think about the possibilities; maybe I should say children don't put limits on what is possible. Children are less likely to analyze their relationships with others or speculate on how relationships could be improved.

Judgment comes in many forms, but the pressure of it results in what we consider "normal." In our traditional society, little boys put on the mask of masculinity. Little girls learn to love dolls and pink. Those from another culture learn to put on the mask of the dominant culture. We want to fit in. We want to be seen as strong or sexy. Some of us even dumb ourselves down so our gifts don't give us away. We want to be accepted by those who may be intimidated by the brightness of our gifts. In school we learn the proper way to carry ourselves. We learn to fit into the box of society that we are expected to fit into—race, gender, sexuality, culture. Even during our religious services many of us wear masks and hide our true selves in the one setting that we should be allowed to be ourselves.

I remember one of the first times I became aware of the mask of masculinity. I was walking with some heavy hymnbooks after church. I was holding the books high to the side of my chest, cradled in my arms, much like one would hold a baby. It was a perfectly stable and comfortable way to carry books, or so I thought. Then someone called me a "sissy," and I was chided for carrying the books "like a girl." I soon realized that in this society, men carry their books in one hand, at their side, no matter how clumsy or unstable that is. I learned also that men are supposed to be interested in having sex with as many girls as possible, to be rough and tough, to play ball and cuss. No matter how I felt about those things personally, if I was to be a proper man, then I was expected to do things a certain way. I began to construct my mask to show the world that I was 100 percent, USDA Grade A male. Even if that may not have been healthy or respectful to females I encountered, I was supposed to live into someone else's image of manliness.

So what are you masking? Most often we mask our imperfections, our weaknesses, and our moral failures. We mask our differences to connect with certain groups, but we also mask our gifts and talents in settings where we believe it is not safe to expose them. In the first chapter I mentioned the false image of social media.

What we post online often reinforces the mask, like a filter on SnapChat. Through our posted images, we pretend to have perfect families, eat perfect food, and have perfect vacations. We wake up with the mask of flawlessness. Very rarely do we present our lives unfiltered. Even the recent flow of unfiltered celebrity photos are carefully crafted, or, in other words, masked. "Supermodel Coco Rocha took to Twitter to show fans that her 'no-makeup' look actually does include the use of makeup. She also insinuates that she's not the only one to do it, saying, 'That "no makeup, effortless" look took about 2 hours and 5 people (including a makeup artist!) to set up.'"[12]

So much time and energy goes into building the mask and comparing ourselves to others that we lose that sense of our true selves we enjoyed as little children. Like the Evil Queen in the story of Snow White, we no longer appreciate our own beauty; it has to exceed the beauty of some societal rival. *There is an ugliness to this, an ugliness that says our true self can only rise at the expense of another.* This attitude tells us, "There can only be one," which is quite impossible in a world of 7 billion people.

Does this mean that your gifts are not special? No, I am just saying that there is plenty of room for us to carve out that IDEAL life. You will drive yourself crazy comparing yourself to others. We will discuss this in detail later in the book. But as a side note for those of you that are being bullied for one thing or another, remember that societal paradigms are really location specific. We live in a big country and a big world. In African countries people carry items on their heads. I have seen women and small children carrying enormous loads for great distances. Carrying stuff on your head is really quite efficient it seems. A number of the people I met in Ghana and Zimbabwe were so skilled that they could balance the load on their heads while doing other tasks because their hands were free. I often wondered why folk in America do not carry stuff on their heads. I think I know the answer: in America people would call you a fool and uncivilized. In Ghana folks would call you, well, nothing, because it is the norm. Take all the criticisms with a grain of salt. The boots that make me look country-dumb in New York City or Chicago are perfectly chic footwear here in Texas or in Oklahoma or Kansas. As you grow and mature, you will have the opportunity to become part of communities that fit who you are.

In a blog post titled *5 Masks We Wear and Why We Should Take Them Off*, Tina Williamson eloquently writes, "Becoming authentic is a process to begin knowing ourselves. To understand our own personality traits, behaviors, values, beliefs, needs, goals and motives. It's having the courage to acknowledge our limitations, and embrace our own vulnerability."[13] We have to face the world without our masks and ponder the reflection that stares back at us.

> **Work on your limitations enough so that they don't hinder your forward progress, but focus most of your energy on developing your strengths.**

Somewhere deep in the annals of history someone came up with the cliché, "Work on your weaknesses." I say that is poppycock. You definitely should *understand* your weaknesses and limitations. But *work* on your strengths and talents. Never hide the things you are great at—let them shine. I spend very little time working on my areas of limitations. I identify what they are and I find ways to address them so they don't get in the way of me becoming who I am called to be. This is not to say you don't try to improve yourself, but work on the areas that make your good *great* and make your great *greater*.

Here is an example: I am not the best grammarian or proofreader in the world, so should I spend hours and hours enrolled in a class to perfect my English skills? (Some of you reading the book may say, "Yes, you should.") I say no. I would rather write and create, and then hire someone or solicit a friend to help me proofread my work. Better yet, today the phrase that pays is, "There's an app for that." Yes, I need a certain level of competency, but I realize my limitations in that area. What if you simply have very little talent for music, but you are gifted in baking? Well, if you were seriously pondering which path to follow, I would advise you that your time would be better off taking culinary arts classes rather than advanced music theory.

Let's look at this by using an example from sports. What if you are a gifted basketball player and you can only dribble with your right hand. Should you work to strengthen your left-hand dribble? Certainly you should spend time to overcome that limitation that relates directly to your strength. What if, when game time comes and you have been working on that left-hand dribble, *but* you have an unstoppable, behind-the-back, through-the-legs dribble using your right hand, wouldn't you dribble with your right hand most of the time? Of course, that's what I would tell you makes the most sense. If you could only go right you would be predictable and the other team would know your one move. Work on your limitations enough so that they don't hinder your forward progress, but focus most of your energy on developing your strengths.

We must first understand ourselves in order to bring about the change to accomplish our goals. Masks obscure our vision, masks slow us down and limit our potential. We gaze in the mirror and reject our limitations and weaknesses as separate from ourselves, instead of acknowledging that they shape who we are.

**Glen's Guidance**

- Don't hide behind the mask. Let the world see the real you.
- Avoid the mask of flawlessness. It is an illusion.
- Focus on your strengths.
- Be patient. Your community is out there.

# NOTES

# Chapter 3

# Who Am I Right Now?

*What am I, who am I, what will I be?*
*Where am I going and what will I see?*
—Glen A. Larson, "Suspension"[14]

This world can quickly become meaningless and empty if we don't understand where we fit in. One of my absolute favorite TV shows of all time is *Buck Rodgers in the 25th Century* with its great theme song "Suspension," performed by Kipp Lennon. The series centers on Captain William Anthony "Buck" Rogers, an astronaut who commands a spacecraft that is launched in May 1987. Due to a life-support malfunction, Buck is accidentally frozen for 504 years before his spacecraft is discovered adrift in the year 2491. The twenty-fifth century scientists are able to revive him. He learns that civilization on Earth was rebuilt following a catastrophic nuclear war that occurred shortly after he was lost in space, and Earth is now under the protection of the Earth Defense Directorate.

The series follows him as he tries (not always successfully) to fit into twenty-fifth century's culture. You can imagine how hard it would be for someone from the 1980s to fit into the twenty-first century iPhone era; imagine how hard it would be to fit into the twenty-fifth century. But Buck is uniquely placed, due to his pilot and combat skills and personal ingenuity, to help the Earth Defense foil assorted evil plots to conquer the planet. Though he is in a different time, Captain Buck Rodgers quickly learns how to take his past skills and transfer them to the future. Sure it is fantasy, but people transfer skills every day in our world as technology changes and new skills are needed in the workforce.

The question we started with was, "Who am I?" Yes, figuring out who you really are can be a challenge. Often we let (or maybe parents and society tell us) our jobs or careers define who we are. But not all people select professions based on their passions.

My dad was somewhat of a jack-of-all-trades, a country Renaissance man. As a child, I was baffled when my father would talk about all the jobs he had held at various times in his life. He'd been a short-order cook, owned a gas station, was a mechanic and a janitor, and even a mortician for a time. He had worn so many hats in his lifetime, and I couldn't figure out why. Why didn't he pick one thing and stick to it?

When I was six years old, I was pretty sure I was going to be a dolphin trainer. If you were kid in the seventies and watched the show *Flipper*, that might have been your dream too. Ask your parents about the show or catch it on YouTube. The main kid in the show, Bud, somehow never had any adult supervision and was always swimming by himself in the ocean with Flipper, his domesticated dolphin. Yes, that was my dream, to be free like Bud chasing dolphins on my surfboard and I was determined to stick with that dream the rest of my life. Now that I am older, I get it. I finally understand my father's career choices. I too have been a number of things in my life and in some ways I am just beginning to embrace my healthy identity and passion. Like my father, I have worn a number of different hats. I am sure you have also.

Who we are in life is as complex and multifaceted as a brilliant diamond. As we think about discovering our call and developing a healthy identity, let's consider our roles. Most of us take on many roles as we encounter others. Our identity is composed of:

- Perceived roles (How we see ourselves)
- Our roles in our family
- Our roles at school and work
- Our roles in society
- How we are perceived by those around us
- Our calling

*We are fearfully and wonderfully made. —Psalm 139:14, author's adaptation*

*You can't look at your life's calling without looking at all of you.* In chapter 5 we will take a deeper look at calling. I want to stress, your calling may not necessarily mean your chosen career or what you do to pay the bills. Sometimes all the things that make up who we are line up very closely. Other times they seem very distinct from one another. We do want to make sure there is a healthy relationship between our call and the other aspects of our identity. We need to get rid of any clutter that prevents us from living out our call.

Many of us grow up thinking we are going to be presidents, princesses, nurses, and firefighters. But childhood dreams don't often line up with what we actually become, e.g. my Flipper story—although I still want to try surfing.

In life, the roles we play are sometimes chosen, sometimes thrust upon us without expectation, or sometimes forced upon us through a series of unfortunate events. Yes, sometimes we choose our roles willingly and other times we fall short of what we hope to be. Various people—our parents, bosses, loved ones, teachers, coaches, and faith leaders—place their expectations on us. Often these expectations are based on *their* dreams and desires and not *ours*. If we are tall, people suggest we play basketball or model, but we may personally desire to be artists or accountants. They suggest we become doctors and lawyers, but we want to work construction or stay home and raise a family. We may seek to work with our hands while their hopes are pinned to our going to college. We long to change the world; others worry about how much change is in our pockets.

Even as a parent I have other parents telling me what my own children's career path should be. It really never ends. My daughter is creative and at this point in her life, she wants to move into a field that utilizes that creativity. Good for her I say. She has a plan, she has done the research and I give her advice as needed, but my friends really want her to be the stereotypical, corporate professional and focus on making money. Well, that is not where she is being called at this point in her life and that is okay. In high school she was involved in theater production. At our local church she helped organize events and helped with the technical aspects of a number of productions. Why would it surprise me now that she would be interested in radio, TV, and film?

Who are you right now? Depending on your age, you might not have had a bunch of jobs, but I am sure you have taken classes and perhaps been a part of extracurricular activities. When examining who we are, sometimes we try to look too far down the road. We want to skip steps and consider only *what we want to be* without looking at *who we are*. The future can be pretty fuzzy and it helps if we have some clarity about our present, not that our current situation should be a limiting factor. One thing to note is that as we grow and mature, our motivation changes. What is relevant today, when you are 15 or 25 years old, might not be relevant when you are 35 or 45. This does not mean that we shouldn't dream, but to successfully map out your journey—any journey—you have to know where you are starting. *Remember—your journey will evolve as time goes on.*

When I was 19 years old and at the United States Air Force Academy, I had to go through a program called SERE, (Survival Evasion Resistance and Escape). The training was to prepare us to survive if our plane ever got shot down behind enemy lines. Part of the training involved reading a map and getting from one checkpoint to the next. If we missed a checkpoint, we risked failing the program or getting lost in the woods. Neither option was acceptable, so my partners and I made certain we got to *where* we needed to be *when* we needed to be there.

In order to get from checkpoint A to checkpoint B, I had to accurately map out the best route by comparing the map details to the landscape surrounding me. I located my starting position based on an assessment of all the clues around me and with a detailed map in hand. My team of three survived the challenges, and we did so even though one of my partners caused a rotten tree to fall upon my other partner's head—twice! Thank God there was no blood, but there was a lot of cussing. I will blame that on the concussion I am sure he had.

Such is life—the unexpected happens. Yes, sometimes in life it takes a tree or two falling on your head to get you back on the right track.

Assessing who you are simply starts off by making a list. This list helps you see what is going on in your life. It is like that map they handed me in the woods during survival training.

I started my own list one day when I sat down and asked myself, "Who am I right now?" The light bulb finally clicked for me that day. To understanding my calling, I had to ask myself, "Who am I right now?" What are the things I am doing in my life that I love and what are the things that I hate?

Once I examined all my past and present roles and all the things I was involved in, I decided that I was tired of doing what everyone else expected of me. I was going to embrace all my gifts, talents, choices, and flaws to become the best me that I could become. I was going to live my IDEAL life.

What do you love? What fills up your spare time? List everything you love to do, write down your hobbies, take note of the areas in which people seek your counsel. What roles do you fill in your life? I truly believe in the saying, "You do what you are."

Make a chart based on the categories I gave you earlier:

- Your perceived roles: How do you see yourself? What roles do you place yourself in that might not fit other categories? Are you an organizer, the fun person in the group, or maybe the sensible one? What do people ask your advice about?
- Your family roles: What is your role in the family? Are you son, daughter, parent, grandchild, sibling?
- Your work/school roles: List past and present jobs and school activities.
- Your roles in society: List clubs, organizations, and faith groups you are a part of. You can even add hobbies.

My lists looked something like this:

### Perceived Roles (How I see myself)

- Leader
- Spiritual advisor
- Organizer
- Amateur chef

**Family roles**

- Husband
- Father
- Financial provider
- Youngest son
- Brother

**Work roles (past and present)**

- Military officer
- Chief operating officer
- Pastor
- Restaurant server
- Starbucks barista
- Event planner/Project manager

**Roles in society**

- Church member
- Volunteer youth worker
- Blogger
- Runner
- Foodie

Ultimately, we are the sum of our choices, our environment, and our opportunities. We have to blend all of that together to become our IDEAL selves. We can't be anything but who we are. Greatness thrives in all of us. An important first step is understanding who you are and growing from there.

## Exercise 1: Create your "Who Am I?" lists

**Reflection questions**

1. What sticks out from the lists that you created?
2. What do items you listed have in common?
3. Do your perceived roles match up with what you are actually doing?
4. How do your work or school roles match other aspects of your life?

**Glen's Guidance**

- Consider your many roles.
- Lists are good—start making one.
- Accept that who you are changes over time. That is normal.
- Start with who you are right now.

# NOTES

_____

_____

_____

_____

_____

_____

_____

_____

_____

# Chapter 4

# I Am Not

*"I am not strange. I am just not normal."*
—Salvador Dali[15]

Don't worry about being considered strange or being called a weirdo. Who notices normal anyway? I love being different. Getting to the point of accepting who you are and finding your IDEAL self is understanding who you are not. Sometimes that can be the most helpful thing of all. Many of us waste so much time trying to copy someone else's IDEAL life that we never find our own. Even if you are an identical twin, you were created as a unique individual. I would venture to guess that even the former *Full House* sit-com twins, Mary Kate and Ashley Olson, seek some sense of personal independence.

> *"For we dare not class ourselves or compare ourselves with those who commend themselves. But they, measuring themselves, by themselves, and comparing themselves among themselves, are not wise."* —2 Corinthians 10:12 NKJV

Don't compare yourself to others. It will drive you crazy.

One of the greatest examples of the pitfalls of comparing yourself to others that I can think of comes from the basketball world. First, let me say, "I'm black and I suck at basketball." Sometimes I am as shocked by that as you. Remember how I told you that I am often the only person of color in many of my educational and professional circles? Well, imagine having people think you can play basketball, and they quickly realize that you don't fit the stereotype. That is one mask that I would welcome, the ability to hoop like the greatest of all time. But, alas, that is not me. I am not even considered the most average of all time at the sport. My ball skills are somewhat laughable.

But Michael Jordan is arguably considered the greatest ever. Since the end of his professional playing career, many sports fanatics have been waiting for "The Next Jordan." They are still waiting even though Jordan has not played basketball since 2003. Today you probably know Jordan more for his shoes than his on-the-court game.

The person who has come closest to being "Next" has been Kobe Bryant. But comparatively, Kobe will always fall a bit short. Why? Because, it is perceived that he intentionally patterned himself after Jordan. Statistically they are very similar players. Kobe has the edge in a few categories; Jordan has the edge in a few. YouTube is filled with Jordan vs. Kobe moves. ESPN has an entire webpage on the Kobe vs. Jordan comparison. Many sports critics agree that Kobe Bryant's career will always be defined by Michael Jordan's. Absent of the Jordan narrative, Kobe Bryant is undoubtedly one of the greatest players ever. Now that he is retired, Kobe will never be able to get that elusive sixth championship ring that would tie him with Michael. Kobe did have *two*, yes *two* of his basketball jerseys retired. My guess is that he did it to one-up Jordan who also wore two numbers in the NBA, but only retired the most famous, #23.

**Work with the tools that God has blessed you with and stop gazing into that unrealistic magic mirror.**

Today, professional basketball stars like LeBron James and Stephen Curry have been able to carve out their own basketball identities although LeBron was highly criticized for not having Michael's win-at-all-cost mentality. It is said that Jordan would belittle and even fight teammates. He demanded people live up to his greatness and if you didn't, you were left out in the cold. Lebron James on the other hand has now become known for his unselfishness and his ability to elevate his teammates to the championship level. His gift is elevating the average players and inspiring them to believe in themselves. Stephen Curry has taken the 3-point specialist to another level and is changing the way NBA teams are coaching the game. Curry is not concerned about Jordanesque dunks, LeBron-like power, or Kobe-like intimidation. No, he has perfected the 3-point shot. His style of play has caused a shift in how teams are built. Stephen Curry has not necessarily pioneered something new, but he is definitely doing it his way.

Early in my career in ministry (since the basketball thing did not work out), I tried to mimic others. I wanted to preach with the fervor of Dr. Martin Luther King, Jr. I wanted to captivate the crowd like black Baptist preachers. I admired their tonality and stage persona, but I quickly found out that my trying to preach like them was laughable. In fact, no matter how much I tried to embrace the Baptist preacher persona, I couldn't pull it off. I just decided to be me. I found my own style with my own rhythm and it works for who I am. People think I am funny, so humor became a part of my style of delivery. Now there was some trial in error in figuring out my style. I even preached with a chainsaw once, but that is a story for another book.

Most people catch on quickly when you try to force yourself into a mold that wasn't designed for you. People spend thousands of dollars and literally risk their health trying to look a certain way, to fit into a certain body image that they will never be able to obtain. According to registered dietician Kari Hartel in the diet and weight loss journal FitDay, "You can't change certain aspects of your appearance that were predetermined by genetics (unless of course you undergo painful plastic surgery). For example, your bone structure, frame size, the areas in which you tend to store extra fat, and your metabolism (to a certain extent) are determined by your DNA. So while you may hate that you have your mother's hips or your grandmother's thighs, these things are likely out of your control."[16]

That does not mean that you cannot be healthy or overcome some bad habits, but you have to be satisfied with becoming the best *you* possible. You may never look like Taylor Swift, have huge muscles like your favorite football player, or be a size 2 model. Work with the tools that God has blessed you with and stop gazing into that unrealistic magic mirror.

The diet industry has preyed on our false image of self to the tune of more than $600 billion dollars.[17] People spend money to buy food, books, and formulas to help them look like the people in the magazines. What we need to keep in mind is that these gorgeous magazine pictures are airbrushed, computer-manipulated images of people who, in real-life, are not nearly as perfect as their photos. Flawless they are not. We have become slaves to the media mirror. The mirror shows us its IDEAL but hides the real truth—these magazine beings do not really exist. They are figments of some graphic designer's imagination.

Why is it important for you to come to grips with who you are not? Having an unrealistic or false self-image will only hinder you as you live out your call—that summons to a particular course of action, influenced by the divine. Chances are if you hate the water, you will not be the next Olympic swimming gold medalist. (Sometimes people are just physically unique. Aside from being comfortable in the water, if you are going to be an Olympic swimmer, it also helps to have big feet and good genetics like Michael Phelps.) If you are afraid of heights, maybe your goal should not be to get a job as a high-rise construction worker. A friend of mine once told me that she dreamed of working in a natural history museum, but her fear of large stuffed birds helped her realize that that might not be her IDEAL path.

Sometimes though, factors that might seem like limitations can be overcome as you begin to live into your calling and start developing a healthy identity. In chapter one, we talked a bit about limitations and working mainly on strengths. But even working on strengths requires hard work and determination. Don't confuse your own limitations with barriers put before you by others because you are different. Sometimes your gifts might not fit the mold that society uses to measure you by. Maybe you come from a poor family. Maybe no one in your family has a college education. Maybe you live in an abusive situation and the people in your life tell you that you will never be better than them or that you will never amount to anything. It might seem like the odds are stacked against you, but you can beat the odds going down a road few are willing to travel. That road takes a great deal of sacrifice and an intense level of intestinal fortitude, a gut check.

For example, the height of the average NBA basketball player is 6 feet 7 inches.[18] If you are significantly under 6 feet, most NBA coaches, general managers, and scouting experts are not going to give you much of a look. In other words, no one will want to draft you. That did not stop Muggsy Bogues at 5 feet 3 inches and Earl Boykins at 5 feet 5 inches from having successful careers and beating the odds. Many people thought their dreams of playing in the NBA were unrealistic. That did not stop them. But, for sure, they did not start playing basketball at 18 and jump to the NBA. No, they played in their neighborhoods challenging their friends and older players. Then they moved to rec leagues, schools leagues, college, and then the pros. At each level their commitment, skills and "gut" were checked. Heck! You want to talk about working hard and pushing to reach your dreams, Earl Boykins's father would sneak Earl into a gym in a gym bag. As a child, Earl Boykins grew up playing in rec leagues with his father and other grown men. Earl and these other shorter players put in hard work and were very successful at lower levels which gave them a true sense of their potential.

In regards to sports, I am a fan. By no means am I an athlete. While the stars I use in some of my analogies were out schooling folks on the playground, I was in the library reading books, schooling my mind. I was going to church summer camp. I was hanging out at church business meetings with my mom. Little did I know at the time those activities were preparing me for what I am doing now: speaking, writing, and leading. To quote a people meme expression, "One does not simply" get on stage to speak to six thousand people without a lot of practice.

But, understand that before people hired me to speak, I gave a lot of free speeches. I can't tell you the number of church dramas I participated in. There were school plays and presentations. There were invitations to deliver Dr. Martin Luther King Jr.'s "I Have a Dream" speech to civic organizations. I think I am most proud of being the voice of the giant in my elementary school production of *Jack and the Beanstalk*. That recitation of "Fee-fi-fo-fum, I smell the blood of an Englishman" made me somewhat famous in my school, but, more importantly, it gave me confidence and a passion for the stage and for addressing crowds.

A crucial step in discovering your call in life or becoming the IDEAL you is taking a self-assessment. Sure it may be easy to see your gift if you are an amazing singer, a phenomenal athlete, or a mathematical genius. But for some of us, finding our gifts can be difficult. After all, we have so many life roles and so many expectations that we might not have the opportunity to develop our true gifts. We might not have a guide or mentor who helps us interpret and clarify our gifts, or we might be one of those multi-gifted folks who are good at so many things they can't decide. This is not just about making a list of everything we do but also assessing how well we do those things.

*What gives us joy?*

*Where do we excel?*

*What do we just plain suck at?*

Unrealistic expectations can consume us and so can unrealized potential. Look at the story of the biblical leader Moses. Moses went from being the child of a slave, to a prince of Egypt, to exiled shepherd, to deliverer of his people. After being displaced from his life of luxury, Moses could have easily folded. He wandered in the desert until coming across the family of Jethro and assuming the roles of husband and shepherd. There is no indication that Moses knew that he would soon be the savior of a nation. He had not yet embraced his divine summons. He had not yet met God, the great I AM (Exodus 3:14). That spiritual experience help Moses realize his own "I AM." Moses got clarity on the mountain top and as you live your life, I hope that you have experiences that give you clarity, that add meaning to your life.

The story of Moses is a great example of how chance and circumstance can shape our identity. I say chance and circumstance rather than destiny or misfortune. I avoid the term *destiny* because the modern usage of the word makes it seem like we play no active role in our success or failures. Some people believe in predestination. People often say, "Well, this is the life God planned for me." But I believe God gives us a choice. We may have all the opportunities in the world thrown at us, but that will not make us successful. While we may have a preordained path in life, we must still choose to walk down that path to get to where God wants us. Just like the GPS in a car. It can give us turn-by-turn navigation, but how many of us ignore it because we know a shortcut? *We often think people achieve success through dumb luck, but luck is the place where opportunity and preparation converge.* Not that I am advocating it, but, heck, even if you win the lottery, someone had to get in a car and drive to the store and purchase the ticket. The luck fairy doesn't just leave winning tickets under your pillow.

Opportunity can strike anytime and anywhere, but "lucky" people are able to leverage the situation for their benefit. Imagine Robin who has saved several thousand dollars. Maybe it took 10 or 20 years for her to accumulate that amount of wealth. Let's say she was working at a $10 an hour job. Maybe Robin worked hours of overtime to have accumulated these savings. Now also consider Perry who makes $60,000 a year and spends every dime he has on flat screen TVs and the latest and greatest gadgets without saving a penny. What if a fantastic investment opportunity comes up for both Robin and Perry? What if a friend has an absolutely foolproof idea that is guaranteed to work, but the friend needs cash to get it up and running? Which one of the people will be the "lucky" one? Well, Robin, of course, the person financially prepared to leverage the opportunity. Preparation is key.

Going back to the biblical story of Moses, we see that Moses was uniquely qualified to lead the children of Israel out of bondage. He had the right ethnic heritage, but he also honed a number of leadership skills while living and working for Pharaoh. These skills made him the perfect ambassador to negotiate the release of the Hebrew captives. Anyone could have walked by that burning bush (Exodus 3:2), but only Moses could fill the requirements of the role of deliver without being consumed. *The Moses story is an interesting one. He could only receive the message from the burning bush after he had been stripped of all the other clutter in his life.* He found his call not in the lush extravagance as a prince of Egypt, but in the uncluttered existence of a shepherd.

*Assessments are a big part of sorting out the truth from the clutter.* Many of us have become compulsive idea and dream hoarders. We peruse social media, pin on Pinterest, and like everything but ourselves. We gather the ideas of others but fail to engage our own calling. We say we want to keep our options open, but we are afraid to step out and risk failure. We are afraid we will lose.

What is compulsive hoarding? According to the International OCD Foundation, compulsive hoarding includes ALL three of the following: (1) A person collects and keeps a lot of items, even things that appear useless or of little value to most people, (2) These items clutter the living spaces and keep the person from using their rooms as they were intended, and (3) These items cause distress or problems in day-to-day activities. [19]

Mental hoarding can be just as damaging as physical hoarding. We can clutter our lives with so much detail and information that we become immobilized and there is little room left for us to pursue our true path. We become hidden under the false images of who others want us to be. We can begin feeling overwhelmed that we don't measure up or that we are inadequate. Some idea hoarders get high on learning the latest thing, or they jump on get-rich-quick schemes before eventually tossing those ideas in the "well, it didn't work for me" pile. At some point, to move forward and find our IDEAL selves, we have to toss out everything that is not us.

Two people can achieve the exact same things, but one can still feel like a failure. It is up to us as individuals to decide our pathways to success. We find our call and understand how to live into it in different ways. That is why I tell people over and over again my golden rule: My IDEAL may not be your IDEAL—and vice versa.

There is no one-size-fits-all method to living this life. Yes, we can glean from the wisdom and experience of others, but eventually we have to put all the pieces together to make it work for who we are. You can apply this to how you live out your calling and how you choose your career.

"Weird Al" Yankovic, a music parody artist, is probably one of the few people I can think have who has had longstanding success based solely on copying others. But he doesn't parody one person. Weird Al's success is not about imitating just one character or artist. He is not an impersonator. He has the uncanny ability to pull from the talents of many successful people. Some impersonators have been successful in the short run, impersonating a single president, a pop star, or the celebrity of the moment. When that person is no longer in office or their star falls, then the impersonator (like the person they are mimicking) becomes irrelevant. We can examine the lives and talents of many people in order to live a life responding to that divinely-inspired summons, but we shouldn't seek to become a carbon copy of anyone.

In chapter three you made several lists related to all the roles that comprise who you are. Use this next exercise to assess your strengths and give yourself a better sense of your call.

## Exercise 2: The Assessment

*Perform at least two of the assessment models in this section.*

### Assessment #1—The Self-Assessment

In chapter one I said the first step in discovering you call or becoming the IDEAL you is making your "I AM" list to see what you are right now. Look at the list you created in the first exercise. As you consider things such as hobbies and clubs or organizations that you are a member of, also consider what can aggravate you.

For example, are you the one who has to fix the table decorations when you attend a birthday party or straighten pictures when you go to a friend's home? Maybe you do so because you are called to be a designer. Do bad processes, systems, and inefficiency bother you to no end? Maybe you are a project manager or process consultant. Do you hate to see people develop unhealthy habits? Maybe you should become a fitness expert, a doctor, or a nutritionist.

Think of an oyster. A priceless pearl is the result of a foreign substance, an irritant slipping into the oyster between the mantle and the shell, which irritates the oyster. It's kind of like the oyster gets a splinter. The oyster's natural reaction is to cover up that irritant to protect itself. The substance used eventually forms a pearl. Sometimes our living into our calling can be defined not only by what we do and enjoy, but by what irritates us as well. Here are four questions to answer as part of your self-assessment:

#### 1. What are your interests and passions? What energizes you?

Begin by asking yourself, "What do I enjoy doing?" Perhaps you like being creative, leading teams, or being outdoors. Life often pulls us in a certain direction. Often we limit our thinking to money. I will challenge you on that. Money is just a means to an end. Money gives us greater access to our interests and passion. We could make all the money in the world, but not have the time to enjoy our lives. That is not the IDEAL life.

## 2. What are your skills? What can you do?

You have many talents and skills, so take an inventory of your abilities. Your unique set of skills may help you find a career, social group, or life path that will allow you to use those gifts constructively. They may be physical skills or people skills. Do people always ask for your advice in a particular area? Are you the neighborhood fix-it person, caretaker, dog walker, or bread baker? These skilled services may give you insight into your call. Maybe you are the person everyone comes to for advice on how to get things done in the community. This might mean you would be a great politician or other type of public servant.

## 3. What are your values? What gives you purpose and meaning?

Think about what you value deeply. Values underpin your actions and the way you feel about work—why you do what you do. Some examples of values might be independence, helping others, or recognition. By understanding your personal values, you will be able to select a path that is in line with how you see the world and what matters most to you. Some people care about the environment. Some people want to save the whales. Other people have a heart for the poor or abused. What we value says a lot about who we are and the path we should follow in life.

I once worked for a national call center. You are probably familiar with them. They sell about 90 percent of the things you see on television late at night: the super knives that cut through steel and tomatoes, the spray that you can use to paint a door screen and turn it into a boat, the pots and pans that you get for three easy payments of $19.95, stuff like that. Upselling is the name of the game. You think you are ordering wax for your car at $9.95 per bottle and you wind up with a $20 a month subscription to some super supreme buyer's club.

The call center I became most familiar with sold magazine subscriptions. Some of them were on the more, let's say, *adult* variety. I wasn't comfortable selling that product or even tricking people to spend additional money on programs and warranties that were attached to many of the products. I eventually left that job because the company's values did not align with mine.

## 4. What type of work environment fits my personality and work style?

Your personality develops from your life experiences and genetics and can influence how well-suited you are to different careers or activities. Finding a career that aligns and fits with your unique personality will allow you to be genuine and fulfilled in your work. Again, not that your working career and your calling are the same thing, but the same principles apply. I would not be a very good veterinarian. I don't really like animals, other than fish, all that much. Both pet owners and I would be sadly disappointed if I had chosen that profession.[20]

### Assessment #2—The Peer Assessment

Ask your friends about your gifts. What do others think you are good at? I add this with some caution. Sometimes we can allow the wrong people to speak into our lives. So we have to use discernment and wisdom when consulting others. Ideally listen to people who have discovered and embrace their call. Consult with people you know and trust. Ask a teacher, a coworker, or trusted friend who knows you well.

### Assessment #3—Personality Assessment

Take a standard personality test. There are many tests available online. Personality tests measure your behavioral style, opinions and motivators—for example, whether you prefer working in a group or independently, whether you prefer taking charge over situations or following others. Personality tests also measure personal attributes such as temperament, career interests and personal values.

There are several popular personality tests which are commonly used. Some measure different personality or behavioral styles from others.

- **The DiSC profile** is a non-judgmental tool used for discussion of people's behavioral differences. If you participate in a DiSC program, you'll be asked to complete a series of questions that produce a detailed report about your personality and behavior. You'll also receive tips related to working with people of other styles. https://discprofile.com/.

- **The Riso-Hudson Enneagram Type Indicator (RHETI**) is the popular Enneagram-based test. The RHETI features a revised edition of the highly popular questionnaire found in *Discovering Your Personality Type*. Rather than just indicating your basic type, however, the RHETI produces a full personality profile across all nine types. This provides you with a unique portrait, indicating the relative strengths and weaknesses of the nine types within your overall personality. https://www.enneagraminstitute.com/.

- **Big Five personality test.** Human resources professionals often use the Big Five personality dimensions to help place employees. That is because these dimensions are considered to be the underlying traits that make up an individual's overall personality. The Big Five traits are Openness, Conscientiousness, Extroversion, Agreeableness, and Neuroticism—or OCEAN. https://www.123test.com/big-five-personality-theory/.

## Assessment #4—Expert Opinion and Research

Seek out a goal model. This is a bit different from a role model. Don't seek to copy or imitate anyone. Remember the Kobe/Jordan analogy? Becoming your IDEAL self will not happen if you are just a poor forgery of the original. But you can look to people who have achieved in areas related to your calling. Maybe you want to be an evangelist and save the world. Read about successful faith leaders such as Billy Graham, T. D. Jakes, or Mother Teresa. You can also reach out to a local pastor who can mentor you and give you insight into the lessons learned. If you think you are called to be a NASCAR driver, then you better head down to a few races, meet the drivers, read up on the history of the sport, maybe even try to find a retired driver to consult with. If you seek advice from experts, you will be surprised how many will spend time with you. Sure, you may get some nos, but that is okay. If you are interested in journalism, the number one reporter in town may not have the time to mentor you, but maybe a younger reporter will and be able to give you more insight into what it is like just starting out.

When you seek out your goal model, remember you are not trying to copy what they do, but you are trying to:

1. Understand how they came to understand their call or career.
2. Get a realistic portrait of the positives and negatives of living out this particular call.
3. Learn the skills required to be successful.
4. Understand the cost of this particular call or career. (Cost is something we will explore later.)

One of the best resources for getting connected with experts is an organization called SCORE. Most cities have a SCORE chapter. SCORE is a nonprofit association dedicated to helping small businesses get off the ground, grow, and achieve their goals through education and mentorship. They deliver services at no charge or at very low cost. SCORE volunteers have expertise across 62 industries and they host inexpensive or free business workshops and webinars (online 24/7). Even if you don't want to start a business, these people can talk to you about various professions.

## Assessment #5—Experimentation

Experimentation is the way that many of us discover what it is that we want to do in life. We try a bunch of different techniques until something clicks. Experimentation may not be the most efficient path to becoming the IDEAL you, but it can be effective. A scripture verse says we should:

*"Test the spirits to see whether they are from God." 1 John 4:1 NIV*

Test your calling. Try various jobs to see how they resonate with that divine summons. Some studies suggest that people will change careers over seven times in their lifetime. College students often change majors after finding out more information related to their first post-high school choice. Initially I thought I was I going to be an electrical engineer, but my first calculus course helped choose a different path. To this day I believe that calculus is demonic math and my poor grade in that course should not count. Actually, this lower level course showed me that engineering was not really what I wanted to do. I could have worked hard and become an engineer, but I realized that sitting around all day figuring out differential equations was not life-giving to me. I am not suggesting that you try every random idea. Consider some kind of method in your madness. Always have a plan for why you are experimenting with something new and get involved only in testing careers or calls in which you have a genuine interest or have researched. Make sure the fit is good for you.

It took me a while to figure out and accept my true calling. I experimented with various career paths, trying to understand how to be successful. *Ironically, no matter my position or job description I always felt that my true calling was to be a mentor to the younger generation and to help my team become more efficient by putting people into the right roles based on their skill sets.* So, when I have been in jobs that were not the best fit for me, I was still able to interject my calling into the situation. I was never as passionate about my daily work as I was about helping the people around me become their IDEAL selves. For sure, I always got my work done with a great amount of proficiency, but that is not what drove me.  Because I have had such a broad range of experiences, I now have a broad range of connections to help me achieve my goals.

For example, I love cooking. Does that mean that I should be a chef? Maybe. I actually thought about that for my career choice and I think I would have been good at it, but it is not necessarily the preparation of food that I love. What I really love is interacting with people. I love the planning, the preparation, and seeing people enjoying the results of my labor. I thought it was the cooking that I loved when in truth it was the process that attracted me. I see many aspects of my call when I plan experiences that nurture and help people grow. Cooking is one way of doing that, but there are many other ways for a single gift to manifest itself. Thinking back to my time in college, at the same time I was testing different professional majors, I was also joining different clubs and activities in college. Interestingly enough I volunteered to plan many gatherings and events while in college. Now I am a professional event planner and speaker, I get paid to do what I was doing in my free time and I love it. Experimentation helped me to understand my areas of passion and skills.

Now maybe you just love lying on the couch. I doubt that being a couch potato is truly what you are called to do. What do you do when you are on the couch? Do you read? Do you watch TV? Do you dream up inventions or create fanciful interior design ideas or write stories in your head? *Your gift is much more than just a single talent; it is how you passionately engage the world.* A passion for talking to people could suggest that you are gifted to be a marketer, a public relations expert, a speaker, or tour guide. Maybe you could even be a social media director though that is more typing than talking. A passion for food could mean you are gifted for nutrition counseling, culinary arts, or competitive eating—you never know. That is why the first step to the IDEAL you is understanding your I AM. When we understand that I AM right now, it helps us to chart out a path of who we are going to be. Over the course of your development, these gifts might get expressed in a number of ways as you gain more experience and you begin to embrace who you really are.

Experimentation is effective because ultimately trying different things can help you sort through the clutter. You can check stuff off your list and say, "Hey, that is not for me." However, experimentation can be very inefficient because it takes time and resources, and you may run the risk of getting distracted as you try and uncover that call buried inside of you. Contrast that with one of my mentees. When she was four years old and the flower girl in my wedding, she told me she was going to be a pastor. I remember her first sermon at 11 years old. She is now in her late twenties and transitioning into a pastoral role. While choosing her IDEAL path, she has had laser focus and vision—something very efficient, effective, and rare.

A friend is a successful pharmacist with a well-paying job that she has prepared for since high school. She has been working as a pharmacist for more than twenty years, but, sensing a call to creativity, she recently took up baking. She has a great paying job, but her fulfilment comes from creating. It is a part of herself that she cannot deny. Even though she is working as a pharmacist, she experimented with various hobbies. She tried her hand at interior design, but ultimately cake baking and decorating captivated her and she is darn good at it. She makes beautiful cakes and many people love her imaginative creations. Now she does have an excellent education and career, but I wonder what her life would have been like if she found this call earlier in life. Twenty years is a long time to try out things, but when you find that niche, waiting all those years may well be worth it for the fulfillment it brings to your life and the lives of others. We can experience aspects of our IDEAL life while working in many areas.

Our calling can be quite distinct from where we work or how we make a living. That is very important to remember as you go through the exercises. Your calling may or may not merge with your career, but as you will read in chapter 5, that career/call combination can play out in a number of interesting ways..

## Glen's Guidance

- Understand what you are not.
- Don't let chance and circumstance define you.
- Do a realistic self-assessment.
- Don't depend solely on luck.

# NOTES

_____

_____

_____

_____

_____

_____

_____

_____

## Part 2

# I DECIDE...

...the path I will follow and how I will respond to life.

# Chapter 5

# Understanding the Call

*So Levi said to Samuel, "Go and lie down again, and if someone calls again,*
*say, 'Speak, Lord, your servant is listening.'" So Samuel went back to bed.*
*And the Lord came and called as before, "Samuel! Samuel!"*
*And Samuel replied, "Speak, your servant is listening."*
*—1 Samuel 3:9-10 NLT*

A friend of mine Del Hershberger understands call. Del directs Christian service
worker programs that connect youth and young adults with opportunities for
international missions and North American volunteer programs. He shares his
thoughts about call, which he refers to as "vocation," in his blog *Vocation and
Occupation: How to Respond to God's Call on your Life*:

> If I had a nickel for every time I've read an article about how to find your
> vocation, I'd be rich. And yet I wonder if they are missing a key point. ... Almost
> every article includes the quote from Frederick Buechner, which goes, "The
> place God calls you to is the place where your deep gladness and the world's
> deep hunger meet." I've seen many expansions on this theme with a Venn
> diagram that shows a small dot at the intersection of your gifts, your passion,
> the world's need, and a way to pay your bills. And I've witnessed many young
> adults immobilized by the multitude of occupational choices that will get them
> most perfectly to that tiny place at the center that is supposed to represent
> your truest calling from God —your vocation. ...
>
> I'm often reminded of a friend of mine who talked about his father working in
> a foundry all of his adult life. It was hard work that he hated. But every day, he
> shared God's love with his coworkers and was a pastoral presence in that place.
> He was stuck in a horrible occupation, but that was where he lived out his
> vocation. And when he retired, dozens of people showed up to tell their story
> about how he encouraged them, mentored them, loved them, and helped
> them to find their God-calling.
>
> I think where we often get this whole conversation wrong, is that we mistake
> our occupation for our vocation (calling). I hope everyone finds an occupation
> that they are good at, enjoy, are needed, and that pays their bills. And it would
> be super-cool if that occupation matches up perfectly with God's call on their
> life. But I hope people will stop obsessing about how to make their living from
> their vocation (calling).

Keith Graber Miller, a Goshen (Indiana) College professor, tells the story of a 16th-century Anabaptist who clarifies the difference between occupation and vocation when he says, "I am a follower of Jesus Christ. That is my vocation. I make my living as a cobbler." Our vocation is how we live out our faith in whatever place we find ourselves—in whatever occupation that might be. [21]

At some point we all have to decide the path we are going to take. After all the self-assessment, the experimentation, and external guidance, we have to decide what is important and in which direction we will start our journey. I have always loved biblical stories where God just tells people, "Go and do this." Life would be so much easier if we all could hear the audible voice of God when we had big decisions to make. There is no bigger decision than figuring out what you are called to do. No pressure, right? Some of us have become immobilized by that decision. But we have multiple opportunities to assess this, and later on in this chapter we will do that more in depth. The other thing we also need to understand is that God might call us to different roles at different times. To everything there is a season (Ecclesiastes 3:1), so we have to keep moving. We don't want fear to stop us from answering our call.

Our calling might not be as clear as the one the prophet Samuel heard from God, but at some point we all must say yes to our calling if we want to feel successful and fulfilled. A single calling can lead you down many paths. It is important to recognize and respond to your true calling and not get distracted by every bright and shiny opportunity that comes along. Your calling tugs at you. It keeps you awake at night. It drives you. It gives you passion. It is that idea that is hard for you to shake. So what are you called to do?

Everyone has a unique story of how they got to that IDEAL place. Let's consider the stories of some historic figures to see how they began to live out their call, which in many cases had nothing to do with their day-to-day occupations.

**Rosa Parks** became the catalyst of the Civil Rights Movement because she was tired—not just physically, but tired of the oppression her people had endured. "People always say that I didn't give up my seat because I was tired, but that isn't true," she said. "I was not tired physically, or no more tired than I usually was at the end of a working day. I was not old, although some people have an image of me as being old then. I was 42. No, the only tired I was, was tired of giving in."

*What are you tired of? Can it be the catalyst you need to cut through life's clutter and find where you need to be?*

**Samuel** the prophet not only heard the voice of God but had a mentor in Eli who helped Samuel interpret what he had heard. He had a mother, Hannah, who had a plan for Samuel from the beginning. She nurtured the gifts she knew he would have. "Sir, do you remember me?" Hannah asked. "I am the very woman who stood here several years ago praying to the Lord. I asked the Lord to give me this boy, and he has granted my request. Now I am giving him to the Lord, and he will belong to the Lord his whole life." (1 Samuel 1:26-28 NLT) And they worshiped the Lord there.

*What voices are guiding you?*

Again many voices will try to guide us and if we are not careful, we can say yes to the wrong people and the wrong things. Be wise in who you allow to speak into your life. Make sure they have achieved the goals they are preaching to you or at least some measure of success. Sometimes you can learn from people who have had failures so that you don't make the same mistakes.

**Bill Gates** as a teenager partnered with his friend Paul Allen to create computer programs and business opportunities at their Seattle preparatory school. Bill enrolled in Harvard to become a lawyer, no doubt influenced by his lawyer father. Eventually both men dropped out of college and turned their passion into a billion dollar empire.[22]

There are some stories that Bill Gates and Paul Allen worked 16-hour days and sometimes forgot to shower in the early days of Microsoft. These men were driven and announced successes even before they happened.[23] For years Bill and Paul sought perfection as they pursued their technological dreams. They decided early on they were committed to success. I would encourage you to read more about these guys and others like them who transformed the computer industry. See the places that drive and belief could take you. Bill was not seeking to become a billionaire. That was just a by-product of him living into his call.

*What drives you?*

**Curtis Martin**, a professional football running back played in the NFL for 11 years, but Curtis did not see football as his true calling. It was not his purpose for living. The foundation he set up supports single mothers, children, individuals with disabilities, and those on low incomes. During his Hall of Fame enshrinement speech, he said,

> At my eulogy, I don't want my daughter ... to talk about how many yards I gained or touchdowns I scored. I want my daughter to be able to talk about the man that Curtis Martin was. How when she was growing up, she looked for a man who was like her father. That he was a man of integrity, a man of strong character, and a God-fearing man. That's what I want."[24]

Curtis Martin is a perfect example of how one aspect of our life can facilitate success in another area. Football was a means to an end for Curtis. His occupation of football allowed him to live out this calling. For Curtis, his purpose was to change the legacy of abuse and poverty in his community.

*What opportunities are available to you?*

Living the IDEAL life doesn't mean that you have it all together. Sometimes achieving our dreams means pushing through rejection, pain, and specific issues. J.K. Rowling[25] wanted to be a writer at the age of six, but it would not be until she was 31 years old that her first *Harry Potter* book was published. In between that time she had various jobs, married, divorced, and lived on welfare. Yet, she kept writing. Before the success of *Harry Potter,* Rowling dealt with a sick mother, a poor relationship with her father, and financial trouble.

Rowling was diagnosed with clinical depression which she claims gave her inspiration to create the Dementors in the Potter series. She dealt with clinical depression and insomnia, but these troubles in her life helped her to create several characters in her book, a book that started as an idea on a napkin.[26] J.K. Rowling had a story inside of her that one day, while waiting for a delayed train, she decided to let out. And although numerous publishers rejected the book, she was determined to share her story with the world.

*What stories are inside of you?*

The decision to invest in your IDEAL life does not instantly guarantee success. It may take days, months, or even years for you to see results. Your life will be filled with ups and downs and even doubts. You have to commit to your decision and have patience. Success follows hard work and persistence.

I joined the military to get a good education and learn some important life skills, but being a career soldier was not my calling even though graduating from the United States Air Force Academy gave me a good shot at it. I was led down another path.

*Deciding means having a plan and knowing how to leverage the opportunities that you are afforded in life.*

Once we understand our life's calling, we still have to live it. We have to decide to accept the challenge of living into our IDEAL. There is a popular saying that proclaims, *"Knowing is half the battle."* I would add that *"believing you can"* is the other half of the battle. Believing might be the most important aspect of living out your life's purpose and finding a healthy identity in the midst of the clutter.

Some people have succeeded because they did not know any better. They were too ignorant or naïve to understand that under ordinary circumstance they should not have succeeded, so they did the extraordinary. Fear is often the blanket that we allow to cover who we are and what we are truly capable of. Human beings were foolish enough to believe that we could fly like the birds. We were even more foolish to go beyond that. We decided one day that we could reach the moon. As President John F. Kennedy said in his famous speech seven years before the first flight to the moon, "We choose to go to the moon in this decade and do … other things, not because they are easy, but because they are hard, because that goal will serve to organize and measure the best of our energies and skills."[27] I think I am particularly fond of this speech, not because it was given in my hometown of Houston, Texas, but for what lies at the heart of the message. We reached the moon first, because we believed that we could. Spurred on by that belief, our country then put a plan in place to turn that belief into reality.

- Can you think it?
- Can you believe it?
- Have you decided that you are going to be successful?
- Do you believe you will live a life of purpose?

President Kennedy also challenged the nation in this historic speech by saying, "If this capsule history of our progress teaches us anything, it is that [humankind], in [its] quest for knowledge and progress, is determined and cannot be deterred. The exploration of space will go ahead, whether we join in it or not, and it is one of the great adventures of all time, and no nation which expects to be the leader of other nations can expect to stay behind in the race for space."[28] Life will go on and progress will be made whether we get on board with the program or not. Our desire and determination can carry us a long way if we are willing to change our mindset and participate. You have as much right to life and success as anyone. The moon is no closer or no further for you than it is for anyone else.

In this life, *we do what we are and we are what we think*. In order to move forward and answer the call, we have to decide to do it. As young children, we think anything is possible. We have limitless potential until time and circumstance begin to ground us. Our formal and informal education is more about what we cannot do than what we can do. We learn to restrict our thoughts which limits our actions, sometimes in healthy ways and other times in very negative ways. Pain teaches us that we should not touch a hot stove so we learn to be careful with hot objects. The pain of falling reminds us to wear proper protection when participating in dangerous activities. The memory of pain can keep us safe and healthy.

But if we are not careful, pain can also keep us from becoming our IDEAL selves. We may bear the emotional pain of racism or gender oppression. We may have been bullied, beaten, or shamed. This emotional pain makes us believe that we are less than we are and incapable of achieving anything significant in our lives.

*If we do not decide to move forward, we are stopped from even trying to live out a life of purpose. Instead, we simply try to survive.*

We have to learn to believe in ourselves and come to the realization that becoming our IDEAL selves is not about what others think, but about understanding our I AM and judging ourselves not by the standards of others. We are not all called to be rich, athletic, or famous. We may never have 100,000 likes on social media. We many never fly to Paris on a G6 private jet, but that does not mean we are not successful and living out a life of meaning.

There are not small gifts. Every gift and calling has value. Dr. Martin Luther King Jr. said it best:

> If it falls in your lot to be a street sweeper, go on out and sweep streets like Michelangelo painted pictures; sweep streets like Handel and Beethoven composed music; sweep streets like Shakespeare wrote poetry; sweep streets so well that all the host of heaven and earth will have to pause and say, "Here lived a great street sweeper who swept his job well.[29]

Dr. King's speech about the street sweeper is right on target. We might be called to be a street sweeper or a street designer, but whatever our call, we need to do our best. We need to illustrate the IDEAL. There is no shame in picking up trash. Every home in America has a trash can and puts out garbage that needs to be disposed of. The waste management industry employs millions of people and generates billions of dollars in revenue annually. Somewhere a garbage man, a street sweeper believed there was profit to be made in trash. One family started hauling trash using carts for a couple of bucks a load. They turned that dream into a company called Waste Management. Waste Management now has annual revenue of over billions.[30]

## Exercise 3: Discerning the Call

If you'd like some concrete ways to test what God might be showing you about your vocation, start with these five tips for discerning call, by Chris Morton, from Missio Alliance:

1. <u>What is one thing that you have consistently been complimented for over the years?</u> These compliments, both direct and occasionally backhanded, are a major clue to our vocation. They reveal how others see us, and the abilities and skills we may not know we possess.

2. <u>What makes you angry?</u> Not a silly frustration, but a righteous anger? It might be interpersonal: the way you see people treating each other. It might be systemic: the problems a community, workplace, or family struggles to solve.

3. <u>What work is so engrossing that you lose track of effort or time?</u> What puts you "in the zone" is unique, but the experience of it is not. It's a powerful sense of meaningful work, concentration, and mastery that most people only experience occasionally.

4. <u>What are you good at?</u> These may be skills you've always had a knack for. You might have learned how to do something as a kid, and pull it out every once in a while. Consider the things that you can do naturally, without even thinking about it, and how you might be able to use that to serve bigger purposes!

5. What high and low points do you remember? As we tell our stories, the high points and low points help to identify who we are. High points show you what you are at your best. Low points can help you realize what you should stay away from. [31]

**Glen's Guidance**

- Your occupation and call (vocation) can be two very different things.
- Every gift and calling has value.
- The things that we are intolerant of are often the problems we are best at solving.
- Look for the opportunities in your life.
- We do what we are and we are what we think.

# NOTES

# Chapter 6

# Understanding the Costs

*Whatever lifestyle we choose to embrace has its price.*
*Forget the free lunch. Nothing in life is free.*
*There is a price to pay for everything, even if it is a hidden cost.*
*—Shannon Skinner* [32]

After you decide where it is that you want to go, ask yourself this question, "Am I willing to pay the price?" Even for the most gifted of us, there comes a point where our natural ability isn't enough. There is a price to be paid if we want to move from the mediocre to our IDEAL. There is a cost to reaching our dreams. Opportunities are not free.

Dreaming of teaching? You may touch many lives, but the pay may not equal the hours you put in or ease the frustration with governmental controls that regulate what you can teach.

Dreaming of the medical field? You can save lives, but you will lose some also. You may also find the costs of education and time extremely high.

Dreaming of social work? The pay in this field is low compared to the amount of work you are expected to perform. The work can also be emotionally exhausting as you help people in various life struggles.

Dreaming of being a stay-at-home parent? The great part is that you get to be with your child and family every day. The downside is that you get to be with your child and family every day. Life could get a little monotonous. Transitioning back into the workforce could be challenging.

Dreaming of being an athlete? I read an article recently about Jackie Stiles, former women's pro basketball player from Kansas. At one point she was the second-highest-scoring NCAA Division I women's basketball player by career points (3,393). Stiles was done with her playing career at an early age because of overworking her body. She had 13 surgeries in four years![33]

It takes practice, practice, and more practice to be an athlete and sometimes the cost is your physical and mental health. You may get the keys to the kingdom as they say. People will envy you, and night after night they may shower you with applause, but the career of an athlete is short and as many professionals find out, one cost of being a professional athlete is old age filled with pain and possible neurological damage.[34]

Often when folks imagine their IDEAL, they go straight to the end result and forget the journey that it takes to get there.

I heard a story at summer camp when I was a teenager. I call it "You Gotta Be a Monk." Here is my version of the story:

### You Gotta Be a Monk

There was this young man living in the old country. Each morning the young man would hear this noise in the distance.

*Do doot do doot doo doot doo doot do doow.*

Without fail, each morning as the sun broke over the horizon, the young man heard the same tune.

*Do doot do doot doo doot doo doot do doow.*

As he grew, he asked his father about the sound. His father explained, "Son, it is the sound of the monks who live up on yonder hill." (They used words like *yonder* in the old country.)

When the boy became 18, he said to this father, "Father, I am going to find the monks up on yonder hill. I must know what that sound is." The young man set off on his journey down toward the distant hills as the melody echoed through the valley.

*Do doot do doot doo doot doo doot do doow.*

The boy walked day and night, through rain, sleet, and snow. After three weeks he arrived at the gates of the monastery. He begged the watcher at the gates, "Oh, most noble monk, what is that sound that comes from beyond your walls?" The monk quickly replied, "My son, the secrets that lie beyond these walls are for those who have consecrated themselves and committed themselves to our order. If you truly desire this knowledge, you must become a monk."

"I am ready," replied the young man. So for two years the young man worked, studied, and did monk-like chores. Each day as he worked and studied, he would see the senior monks line up in the great hall. As he peered through the window, he could see them standing with a radiant glow on their faces as they prepared for entry into the inner room. One by one, they would grab the brass ring of the door and march into the secret inner room. The strange sound would echo through the hall and cause the window to vibrate. The noise that he heard as a child continued to echo in his head.

*Do doot do doot doo doot doo doot do doow.*

Finally, after two years of training, meditation, and silence, the young boy emerged as a monk. He asked the senior monk if he could enter the great hall to see what lies behind the doors with the polished brass rings. The senior monk replied, "My young monk, you may enter into the great hall, but you are not yet ready to go behind the doors." You must consecrate and prove yourself for five more years.

So, for five years the young monk trained, meditated, and watched from inside the Great Hall as the senior monks did their rituals. The noise from behind the great wooden doors rang through his soul, day after day. How anxious he was as he swept and did his daily chores faithfully, counting down the day until he would become a senior monk.

*Do doot do doot doo doot doo doot do doow.*

Eventually the years ticked by and finally it was the young monk's turn. For hours he waited in line; monk after senior monk went inside the great wooden doors only to emerge minutes later, glowing with a Shekinah glory that comes only from someone who has truly experienced the wonders of the cosmos. The clock ticked and the line inched forward as each new senior monk slid forward at the pace of molasses on a cold Sunday morning. Each time the door opened, the cells of the young monk's soul reverberated, down to the sub-atomic level, to the beat of the sound.

*Do doot do doot doo doot doo doot do doow.*

As he reached the door and nervously moved his hand to touch the great brass rings, the sound got louder and louder, or maybe it was his heart beating. He wasn't sure if it was perspiration or anticipation that ran up and down his spine, chilling him to the core.

*Do doot do doot doo doot doo doot do doow.*

The monk threw open the great doors with all the passion of someone who had waited years to begin his journey. He thought about the seven years he toiled as a monk, learning, training, doing chores. Finally, his moment was upon him. He opened the door wide with his sweat-moistened hands fused to the brass rings, and do you know what he saw inside the great room?

Well, I actually don't know. Neither you nor I paid the price to see what was behind that door. You gotta be a monk to find out. (Not the answer you wanted or expected, I am sure.)

In order to reach our dreams and to live out our call, we have to be willing the pay the price, just like the monk in the story. There are no shortcuts. Even though many of us hoped we would find out what was behind the door of the monastery, how many of us would be willing to give seven-plus years to find out? Not many of us. But to achieve our IDEAL or to answer our call, we have to put in the work.

Remember those questions we ask high school graduates? "What are your plans?" "What are you going to do with the rest of your life?" I remember when I was 18 and people asked, "Glen, tell me how you are going to spend the next 50 or 60 years of your life. We know you just finished high school, but what is your plan?"

**A lot of things go on in the background on our journey to success. It doesn't happen overnight.**

To be honest, like many of you, I was just happy to graduate. I was just happy to be able to leave home. But I did not have plans beyond the summer. I knew what was expected of me. I knew what failure would look like, but I had no sense of what it would mean to live out my dreams. Some of my classmates had plans. Some even went on to do the things they dreamed about doing their entire four years of high school. Most of us didn't. I wanted to make a lot of money and graduate college, but I did not have a clear vision of how that would happen. Like many Generation X kids, I was just going to follow the formula that was laid for me and take my chances: Good grades + College = Good Paying Job.

But I soon found out that living a life of purpose and living out your true calling in life is about more than money and some corporate formula. How many people dream of sitting in a cubicle 40-plus hours a week shuffling papers? Not many people I know, and especially not many people who grew up in the twenty-first century.

Even as a student at the Air Force Academy, I dreamt of becoming an electrical engineer until I faced the nightmare of calculus. That one class altered the course of my life and pushed me into becoming a business management major. I quickly realized that I would not become an engineer. While I was smart enough to become one—I eventually got an A- in Calculus I the second time I took it—I knew that I was not willing to take more calculus courses and put in the time that it would take for me to be successful.

Some experts suggest that it takes at least 10,000 hours to become an expert in any given field. The widely touted theory, highlighted in a 1993 psychology paper and popularized by Malcolm Gladwell's book *Outliers*, says that anyone can master a skill with 10,000 hours of practice. But recent studies[35] suggest that even 10,000 hours is not enough time. So one question you have to ask yourself as you launch out on this journey of becoming is, "Are you willing to pay the price to be the thing that you want to be?"

- To be a general surgeon, you will need 10 to 13 years of education after high school.
- To be a professional football player, you will spend 20 hours per week training for three to four years to be considered for a career that on average lasts three to six years.[36]
- To be a pastor in a mainline denomination, you will need six to seven years of education after high school.
- To be a professional musician or entertainer, you will need years of lessons and may spend weeks on the road away from home.
- To be a celebrity, you will lose your sense of privacy.
- To be a fashion model, you likely will be forced to maintain an unhealthy body mass index (BMI).[37]
- To become a police officer, you will risk your life every single day.

If you sit and watch enough reality TV, you can start to believe that all the world's problems can be solved in 60 minutes. We are lulled into believing that this scripted reality drama is a reflection of real life, but it isn't. In these shows people rise from famine to fortune in a few short weeks. Every show is filled with excitement, heartbreak, and some astounding resolution that wraps up the event's day like a Christmas present.

Our real lives are not that neat. A lot of things go on in the background on our journey to success. It doesn't happen overnight. Hours and hours and years and years of practice are involved in perfecting our craft, no matter what that craft is. You ever think about how long a year is? The song "Seasons of Love" featured in the musical *Rent* states it very clearly, "Five hundred twenty-five thousand six hundred minutes."[38] That is one full year broken down in minutes (more during a leap year, of course) and that number should make us all sigh deeply. Each day, each of us is given 24 hours or 1,440 minutes to work on who we want to become. That is basically 43,800 minutes a month that we have can use to accomplish our goals.

**Glen's Guidance**

- You have to be willing to pay the price to achieve in life.
- You have to put in the hard work to unlock the secret behind doors.
- Time is the most precious resource we have.
- If you want to go behind the door, you gotta be a monk. ☺

# NOTES

## Part 3

# I EVOLVE...

...to stay relevant in a dynamic and sometimes unpredictable world.

# Chapter 7

# Time for Change

*"There is nothing noble in being superior to your fellow man;*
*true nobility is being superior to your former self."*
—*Ernest Hemingway*[39]

We are dynamic beings. With each phase of life we reexamine our reason for being. To stay relevant, we must adapt to growth and change.

There is an old saying, "Change or die." Change is going to happen whether we want it to or not. If we stop growing and changing, we become stagnant and rot, or we get stuck in a meaningless cycle, going nowhere, like caged hamsters on a wheel. We are not fulfilling our purpose in life if we are going in circles. Living a life of purpose and achieving your IDEAL is not about reaching a specific point in your life and shouting, "I have arrived!" When we stop growing and progressing, we die—maybe not physically, but emotionally and spiritually, which can be just as bad. According to the Oxford English Dictionary, life is "The condition that distinguishes animals and plants from inorganic matter, including the capacity for growth, reproduction, functional activity, and continual change preceding death."[40]

Anything alive shows signs of growth. People who live a life of purpose continue to stay relevant and continue to grow. As living beings, we must continually reproduce ourselves through our work and through those we mentor. We must also continually deal with the ever-shifting circumstances of life.

We have to evolve.

What is evolution? Here is the non-scientific definition: "It is the process of change in a certain direction."[41] Typically that means going from a simple state to something more complex. Mountains have a very slow evolutionary process. Trees evolve seasonally and at a much quicker pace. As we examine becoming our IDEAL selves, we also must be aware that we cannot become stagnate once we hit our pinnacle. If we are a Shakespearian actor or a nuclear physicist, we will not evolve in the same way as a computer engineer or a musical artist. But we will still evolve. We must continually improvise, adapt, and overcome to stay relevant. The journey from just basic living to our IDEAL self means developing a level of maturity and complexity in our lives that will help us truly embrace who we are. As we evolve, the direction we head should move us closer to the milestones (progress markers) we establish. Our lives should be going from one state of being (our current state) to a better state of being (the IDEAL life).

Think about your relationships in life. Do you have kindergarten classmates you still keep in touch with? (No, the occasional social media interaction does not count.) Not many of us do, at least not in significant ways. We grow up and we move on. We get new friends. If we still maintain close relationships with childhood friends, hopefully those relationships have evolved overtime. Your relationships at age 15 or 20 can't be the same as when you and your friend were nine years of age. If you and your friend are still playing with your Barbie dolls or your Hot Wheels cars, you may want to reexamine your goals and get some new hobbies.

> **The world around us forces us to reexamine who and what we are called to be and forces us to evolve.**

That is why it is important for us to set milestone goals. Most of us have heard of long-term and short-term goals. Our short-term goals should be very short. We should also have daily goals, weekly goals, monthly goals. A successful business owner knows how much revenue the business will generate each hour it is open. We can apply that same principle to our lives. In order to lose weight, you can't drop 100 pounds in one hour or even one month. You have to have a structured eating and exercise plan that takes into account each meal of the day. If you want to write a novel, 60,000 words don't magically appear on the page. You might have to set a goal of 500 words a day; then after 120 days you will have your novel. I recommend setting no more than two to three milestones at a time. This will allow you to evolve in a consistent, manageable way.

Living your IDEAL means staying relevant. As we get older, it is easy to feel like we are useless. We can get stuck in the good old days. *Many people never progress beyond the glory or pain of high school.* This reminds me of the old TV show *Married with Children*. The main character Al Bundy, played by Ed O'Neill, was a salesman for women's shoes (not his dream job). Al frequently told tales of his high school football days, most notably the time he scored four touchdowns in a single game for the 1966 Chicago All City Championship Game. He blamed the outcome of his life on his wife and the "Bundy Curse."[42]

The real world has many "Als." They have become stagnant. They talk about what they *used to be* and blame others for why they have not progressed further. They are just unwilling or unable to change. A person who constantly lives in the past has not evolved. I don't believe that we were created to be temporarily relevant in this world. The world around us changes and we must too. Hopefully if you are a high school student or young adult reading this book you are not reminiscing about the good old kindergarten days. I know the milk and cookies were nice. Sometimes I long for naptime, but I don't think sleeping on a cot listening to "The Wheels on the Bus" is gonna help me now that I am an adult. Plus if my memory serves me correctly, those thin kindergarten mats are not going to support this body of 40-plus years.

Consider for a moment the steel industry in America. Cheaper foreign steel has replaced American steel. Technology and imports have forced people to evolve. Now machines, not people, are working in many factories. Workers have had to retrain or they have wound up unemployed or in low-wage jobs.

"In 1990, the manufacturing industry was the leading employer in most U.S. states, followed by retail trade," according to the U.S. Bureau of Labor Statistics. "In 2003, retail trade was the leading employer in a majority of states. By 2013, health care and social assistance was the dominant industry in 34 states."[43]

The world around us forces us to reexamine who and what we are called to be and forces us to evolve. To realize the importance of change and staying relevant, one can look at the 2012 and 2016 presidential campaigns. Though their politics were very different, both Barak Obama and Donald Trump ran campaigns against the status quo. Both ran on change, promising to take the country in a different direction. Both won their presidential elections.

There are many ways to express who we are called to be. A single gift can manifest itself in numerous ways. A gifted athlete born in Nigeria might become a star soccer player, but had he been born in the United States he might have become a professional basketball player. Just ask Hakeem Olajuwon. The future NBA player and Hall of Famer didn't play basketball until he was fifteen. He was a soccer and handball player as a student at the Muslim Teachers College in Lagos, Nigeria. Given the opportunity to play basketball for the University of Houston, Hakeem was able to translate his athletic ability in soccer to becoming a basketball legend.[44] The gift of and passion for athletics was always a part of who he was. Had not he been given the opportunity to come to the United States, The Dream, as he was called, would likely have had a successful, if not legendary, soccer career.

I often imagine life like a surfer riding the big waves in Hawaii, paddling out each day to see what the ocean is like. At times the ocean is calm. At other times it is a raging monster. Sometimes a big wave knocks you off the board, but you have to get right back on it, knowing that the stability of the shore is just at the end of the ride.

Yes, life is a series of ups and downs. Your path to the IDEAL most likely won't be a straight line. It won't necessarily be 100 percent smooth. Like a surfer, you are going to have to make course corrections. But if you develop the right habits, maintain a positive mental attitude, and have faith, you can hang on and have a wonderful ride—a stable and rewarding life.

**Glen's Guidance**

- Growth is a sign of life.
- As you mature, you should evolve.
- Life is series of ups and downs so hang on and develop the right attitude and skills to stay relevant.

# NOTES

# Chapter 8

# Knowing When to Change

*Change will not come if we wait for some other person or ... some other time.*
*We are the ones we've been waiting for.*
*We are the change that we seek.*
—*Barack Obama*[45]

Follow your nose. That is the best advice I can give you about change. When things in your life begin to stink, you know it is time for change. As a dad, I could always tell when it was time to change a diaper, not just a poopy diaper, but any diaper. The smell alerted me even before the cries began. My wife makes fun of me because I smell my clothes before I put them on. "Why are you smelling your clothes?" she asks. I say I want to make sure they are clean, that I did not mix up my dirty socks with my clean ones. Maybe this is a sign that I need to be more organized, but my system works and I bet some of you do the same thing. The nose never lies. And even though she makes fun of me and my clothes, I often find my wife checking out the milk or the leftovers in the fridge with her nose. Why? Because the nose knows when change is needed.

What is your nose telling you about your situation? Does it smell like rotting flesh or spoiled fruit? In his famous poem *"Harlem,"* Langston Hughes asks, "What happens to a dream deferred?"[46] Does it become a dangerous infection? Does it become a burden that weighs us down?

When our situations become bitter, when our attitude begins to stink, we should consider making a change. I am not only referring to toxic and dangerous situations which have a clear and distinct aroma. I am also referring to when the stench of discomfort becomes consistent and lingers in your life. *Too often we fail to make changes when we should. We wait until our lives fester like a wound.* We then begin to spread contempt and anger within our circles. We fail to become the best of ourselves. Instead, we become the worst of ourselves.

Some people never seem to change. According to a study, "American Mobility Who Moves? Who Stays Put? Where's Home?," one in four Americans will never leave their hometown.[47] A good number of people will never move out of state. They grow up and die in the same neighborhood, work in the same city, and never leave the safety of the familiar. Don't get me wrong; it is okay to be what others consider average. Remember, you set the standard for your own ideal life. Not everyone is called to be the boss or has the desire to travel the world.

I have worked with people who have been in the same role for 20 or more years. They are perfectly content and very good at what they do. Has their job stayed exactly the same in those 20 years? Hardly. Some have had to change job descriptions, where they work, and with whom they work. They have had to learn new technology and new ways of doing things. Imagine being a secretary using carbon paper to make multiple copies of a letter in the 1970s to being in that same role in the 2000s using a laser printer and email. So even though their job titles remained pretty constant over two decades, many aspects of how they work have changed.

We all must change in order to stay relevant in our particular roles. Change is relative. It does not always require a massive shift. It can be incremental over a long period of time or exponential over a very short period. We have to use wisdom and evaluate our needs and the circumstances to determine the appropriate change response.

Here are a few signs that will tell you it is time to make a change in your life:

1. You continue to romanticize the past and are unable to focus on your present situation.

2. You turn down good opportunities out of fear or guilt.

3. You've lost passion for your current situation or are just going through the motions.

4 You become bitter or angry in your current situation.

6. You are unable to perform in your current role or relationship.

7. Your relationships feel superficial or are unhealthy.

8. You have a strong sense that your life or daily routines have no significance.

9. You sense you are compromising your values.

10. Your hobbies and side interests begin to consume more and more of your time.

I have experienced a couple of really significant changes in my life. After I left the military, I worked for a church in Virginia. I was a part of the church for 17 years and a part of the staff for more than 10 years. I basically grew up, got married, and started a family during my time there. My journey with the people in that congregation started when I was a single, 23-year-old and ended with me being a married 40-year-old father of two. It was a great ride. But one day I woke up and realized that it was time for me to make a change. I had changed. My family situation had changed. My dreams had changed.

I wasn't bitter or unhappy, but I realized that I had reached the pinnacle of who I was there. In my ministry role I went from youth pastor to part of the executive leadership team overseeing staff and many of the church operations. There was nothing left for me to do but be senior pastor, a role that was not about to open up and a role that I didn't feel called to. So in order to continue growing and advancing towards my IDEAL life, I packed up my family and moved to Texas. I accepted a new role and I hoped to God that I would not fail. I didn't. Change, though hard and scary, allowed me to spread my wings and fly, much like an eagle getting kicked out of the nest. It was only after leaving the safety of a 10-year career that I began to realize my potential and to truly believe in myself.

I still have very good relationships with my Virginia friends and family. From time to time I still do some work with the church that I left. Advancement and change don't have to be negatives. Sometimes they are very necessary. Even as I write this book for you, I am getting ready for another change. Why? Because I have examined the very list I am sharing with you. I want to keep growing and maximize the life that I have. I am not unhappy or unfulfilled, but as I grow and mature, so do my interests. For me that is enough to know that I need to pursue change.

**Glen's Guidance**

- When things begin to stink, make a change.
- Change is constant, but it is relative.
- When you reach the pinnacle, look for new mountains.
- Change isn't always about being dissatisfied; sometimes it is just about growth.

# NOTES

## Part 4

# I ADVANCE...

...by honing my skills and being the best I can be.

# Chapter 9

# Honing your Edge

*"The thing about a 'comfort zone' is that it sounds, well, just too comfortable—and when you are too comfortable you lose your edge. That's why I call it a comfort pit, because a pit is somewhere you want to get out of as fast as possible."*
— *Bear Grylls*[48]

The learning process never stops. When you think about reaching your IDEAL, the process of evolution (I EVOLVE) is much like sharpening a knife. You take a piece of dull steel to a person who grinds and smooths out the metal until it has an appropriate cutting edge. Typically I am the one in the family called to carve the turkey during the holidays, especially when I hang out with my wife's family. I learned a long time ago to bring my own knives because many people don't have good sharp knives at home. And if I am going carve turkey or ham, I want it to look good like something you see on Food Network. So I have a two-sided sharpening stone with different grits that allow me to keep my kitchen knives sharp. I try to take care of my knives and not let them get too dinged up, so I only occasionally have to sharpen the blades. My honing steel is something I use all the time. A honing steel is that metal rod that chefs clang together every time you see them pull their knives out on television. People mistakenly think the steel is a sharpening tool, but it actually hones a sharp blade.

Advancement is much more like honing a knife. There is a difference between sharpening and honing. Honing is the finishing process where the burrs formed from the sharpening process are removed and a sharpened knife is finished to a fine edge. Honing maintains the edge in between sharpening sessions. Honing does not actually sharpen a knife. Instead, honing straightens, cleans, and polishes the edge of an already sharp knife. Knife edges are very delicate. After just a few uses, the blade edge can begin to actually fold back on itself at a microscopic level. Honing for blade maintenance straightens out the edge and prevents premature dulling of the knife. Technically you should use the honing steel between every few uses. That is how vital honing is. Sharpening can be done once a year. Even after you find yourself living the IDEAL life, you have to maintain your edge. I truly believe that to maintain your edge, you need a mentor. You need professional development. You need a supportive community.

Finding a Mentor

Mentors are wonderful folks. A mentor is someone who agrees to share his/her world with you. A mentor will share skills, knowledge, and expertise. A mentor can also introduce you to other professionals in your field. A good mentor can open doors for you, save you a lot of unnecessary work, help you set career goals, resolve problems, and make sound career decisions. Here are some tips to finding the right mentor:

## 1. Find someone who actually wants to be a mentor.

A good mentor is excited about giving back. Often the mentor selects you and begins the process before you even ask. But other times you may have to cultivate the relationship first. Make a list of what you want from the relationship.

- How often do you want to connect with the mentor?
- What skills do you hope to gain from working with the person?
- How long do you plan for the relationship to last?
- What personality style would you prefer in a mentor?

## 2. Where do you find your mentor?

Look around your current network and social groups. If you are a part of interest or professional groups that relate to your area of interest, then it may be pretty easy to find a mentor with whom you already connect. Common connections make the mentor/mentee relationship easier to manage.

If you have the guts, you can also research mentors with whom you don't have a formal relationship. Social media platforms such as LinkedIn and professional seminars and conventions are great places to start. I met one of my mentors at a convention. She was leading professional development seminars. After sitting in one of her seminars, I made sure I attended every seminar she gave for the rest of the week. After a couple of brief conversations she was willing to meet with me and we have been friends ever since. Sometimes you just have to put yourself out there. Although cold calls can be effective, social media tools work best if you can solicit a warm introduction from someone you know. This helps break the ice and immediately makes people feel like you are in their circle of friends.

## 3. Volunteer

Another great way to find a mentor is to volunteer. Some examples: If you are interested in politics and you want to learn the tools of the trade, work on someone's campaign. If you want to be veterinarian, volunteer at a veterinarian's office. If you want to be a chef, volunteer at a soup kitchen, a restaurant, or at the family cookout. You will be amazed how much people will help you if you help them to achieve their goals.

The great thing about volunteering is that you can usually set up your time as a short-term obligation. Volunteering is the best free education arrangement. And you and potential mentors can check each other out.

Some of my best volunteers later became paid staff or people I still mentor. In fact, one of my best students is a teacher; he was one of the first people I called to read my book and help organize it. Years ago, one young woman and I volunteered together for an event when she was in high school. We were on the same planning committee. Amazingly I eventually hired her to manage the event and seven years later she became one of my employees. This has led to a great mentoring relationship. I was chosen to lead the event because of my years of experience in volunteering for it. Both of us originally volunteered for the event and eventually we both wound up as paid staff leading the event. One reason I hired her was because of the great experience I had with her as a young volunteer. Now she is the executive director of a national magazine. I won't say that was a direct result of my mentoring, but I think that she would agree that being a part of my staff helped her significantly. It gave her the edge she needed to be successful in her executive role.

*A word of caution:* Volunteering to figure out what you are interested in is quite different from volunteering to find a mentor or to hone your skills. Volunteering can also be experimentation, part of the assessment process that we discussed in chapter four. The right type of practice makes perfect, so make sure you take opportunities that will enhance your skills. Volunteering gives you an opportunity to continually practice your gift.

*Another word of caution:* Avoid the suckers who don't really want to mentor you. They just want free labor. Suckers pop in and out of our lives, but when they pop in, they need something. These vampires do their best to suck up all the life-giving energy that you have stored up. They may need your money or your help all the time. They may need you to do their homework or their assigned project. The suckers will drain you to the last drop of life and still ask for more. Who are the suckers in your life? Are they family members, coworkers, so-called friends? Suckers often hang around to glean from the leftovers of your success. Like the old school movie vampires, they feed off you until all your energy is gone.

When I was in high school, I had a friend, Jim, who always needed a ride. "Hey, can you pick me up?" was a familiar refrain. Picking him up wasn't the problem. The problem was that in addition to picking up Jim, he wanted me to pick up his cousin. Jim often wanted me to stop by someone else's house. It was always something extra and Jim never acknowledged the inconvenience or offered to give me any money for gas. The more I gave, the more he asked for. My other friends and I often rotated who drove and who gave money to the driver. Jim was in it for Jim. and after we started asking him to contribute, suddenly Jim moved on to a new crew.

Your time is just as valuable as your mentor's. There should be a *quid pro quo,* an exchange of favors. I had the pleasure of mentoring a seminary student once. The funny thing is that she has more formal education than I do, but I have years more practical experience. We had a wonderful relationship. I provided opportunities and information that helped her obtain class credit. She volunteered to help lead a portion of a program I was planning. It was a win-win. For her, the beauty of it was she knew that when she finished her ministry degree, I would recommend her for any number of positions. For me, she has continued to volunteer with me on occasion and I get to benefit from her training.

Just a last note about mentors. Experience and expertise are far more important than chronological age. One of my mentors is 10 years older than I am; another is 10 years younger. I learn numerous skills and understandings from them, but both are very valuable as I pursue my IDEAL life.

## 4. Professional Development

We live in a world where the final product seems to be the only thing that matters. Any good baker knows that the ingredients and the process are important to the final outcome. Poor ingredients result in a poor cake. Poor process can also ruin the outcome. Our goal is not just to live our lives, but to live our lives well— with excellence and hope. Gathering the right information to be successful is important. We might have to start off by winging it or teaching ourselves, but to truly live into our call at the highest level, we will all benefit from personal development.

Personal development can come in a number of forms. It can come as informal learning from your peers or as formal classes from an instructor. You have to figure out how you learn best. One of the certifications I hold in project management has a whole list of ways I can earn the requisite amount of credits I need to keep my professional credentials. This organization is very specific about professional development, but I am also a member of other professional organizations and from time to time I attend their conventions. Sure they have seminars and keynote speakers, but I learn the most from just talking to peers over meals and in the hallways. I joined the National Speakers Association to launch my career as a paid professional speaker (because my younger mentor told me to). By the end of their first conference I attended, my head was about to explode because of the knowledge I had gained. I was inspired to be better and do better. Also my learning curve was significantly reduced because of the knowledge I gained from people with the same dreams and struggles.

Don't hang around with people who will dull you. Honing your edge means staying true to your dream and surrounding yourself with other sharp people who want to be and do better. People living the IDEAL life need an IDEAL circle of friends. Choose your friends wisely. Avoid suckers and remember those closest to you are often a reflection of you. That is very important for my younger readers. You probably spend more time with friends than you do with your parents or other family members. Choose friends who are at least headed in the same direction as you.

## Glen's Guidance

- Never stop learning.
- Get yourself a mentor.
- Volunteer to get experience.
- Hang out with people who will keep you sharp.

# NOTES

## Part 5

# I LET GO...

...of past hurts, failures, and negative experiences in order to move forward.

# Chapter 10

# Our Past Betrays Us

*Never look back unless you are planning to go that way."*
*—attributed to Henry David Thoreau*[49]

The movie *Kung-Fu Panda II* triggers something in me. Sure it's a kid's movie, but I had a traumatic experience back when the movie first came out. I took my 10-year-old son to see the movie. We had a great time on our father-son outing. We ate popcorn, we laughed, but that day turned out to be one our most meaningful outings, for a very negative reason. I fell.

I am not sure how it happened, but I just wasn't paying attention as we exited the theater with the other guests. One minute I was laughing with my son and half-way watching the credits. The next I was crumpled on the floor in pain with a twisted ankle. By his expression my son must have thought I was having a heart attack. I just needed a second on the floor, first to deal with the pain shooting through my ankle and, secondly, to deal with the embarrassment of falling down in front of the Kung Fu Panda audience. So what was the trauma? For a long time after that I had this intense fear of falling down the stairs. In my mind this simple event that was caused because I was trying to look at the movie screen while walking and talking became a huge issue for me. Sure, the solution was to just pay attention when you walk in a dark movie theater. It should have been as simple as that. But this painful incident somehow rocked my confidence. Over the next few years I became overly cautious when walking down stairs, especially in certain event venues, like theaters.

Many of us fight for our past beliefs, perceptions, and unhealthy habits out of fearful necessity. We construct a mental safe room that keeps us from confronting deeper issues. Without that safe room, we'd have to face the fact that our parents may have been abusive, our country may have a sinister underbelly, our elders may have lied to us, we may be infected deep down with untruths about others, and we may always push others away because we are self-destructive. Who would we be if we were completely open to examine each of our beliefs and let go of them?[50]

You have to let go of the past if you ever hope to move forward and become your IDEAL self. We all handle trauma and abuse differently. We may even have different definitions of what abuse is, depending on our culture and context. *Culture and context always matter. Our North American society is in error when it leads us to believe that we all feel and deal with pain in the same way.* There is no longer pragmatic thought when it comes to how we as individuals are affected by the happenings of life. Everyone is expected to react the same way to situations. *I'd call that a generic categorization of oppression.* This biased theory discounts the distinct experiences of certain groups and individuals while favoring the masses. While it is important that we address the systems and institutions that are harmful and abusive, we can't discount the pain and oppression faced by individuals. No matter how many successful class actions suits we file, no matter how many focus groups we participate in, at some point we as individuals have to deal with our own painful pasts and do whatever we need to do to move forward and claim our IDEAL.

**The past can hold us captive. We may be held hostage by what others have said or done to us or by what we have said or done to ourselves or others.**

Living into your calling means being relevant in the present. One of the shortest passages in the Bible is Luke 17:32: *"Remember Lot's wife."* It refers to the Old Testament story in the book of Genesis where Lot's wife was turned into a pillar of salt for looking back at her old home of Sodom as God rained down fire and destruction. Lot and his wife had been warned by the angels not to look back.

*"When they were safely out of the city, one of the angels ordered, 'Run for your lives! And don't look back or stop anywhere in the valley! Escape to the mountains, or you will be swept away!'" Genesis 19:17 NLT*

Lot's wife turned back. I don't believe that the physical act of turning her head is why God rendered judgment on her. No, Lot's wife was afraid of change. She was either afraid of moving forward to a new future or she was lusting after the comforts of what she was leaving behind.

The past can hold us captive. We may be held hostage by what others have said or done to us or by what we have said or done to ourselves or others.

Today I am a husband and a father. Like many people I did not have the IDEAL childhood. We weren't rich. We were actually kind of poor. By today's standards, my father was physically and verbally abusive. To top it all off, when I was 14 years of age, I watched my father die. When I was in my mid-twenties, I gave the eulogy for my oldest brother, Brian, the alcoholic I mentioned in chapter one. Would either of these events in my life have set me up to be a successful person or have a stable home life today? Hardly. While our pasts clearly shape who we are, we can overcome our negative pasts. I am sure that I carry some scars from my past. I know that it shapes how I make decisions at times and how I interact with people in both positive and negative ways.

Looking back, I know both of my parents loved me. Recognizing the era and culture in which I was raised, I feel good about most of my childhood, though it was far from perfect. Of course today many of the things I experience may be considered abuse, but I was a kid in the 1970s and '80s. Kids got paddled in school and we didn't wear helmets when we rode our bikes. It was a different era. Society has evolved and so have I. Because of that, I would never treat my children like my father treated my brother and me. One time, I remember watching from our kitchen window when my father called my brother into the garage and had him remove his glasses so he could slap him in the face. Head slaps were his go-to move as were his profanity-laced rants and leather belt whippings. These were not just spankings, but true whippings. Getting in trouble with my dad was like inviting a WWE wrestling match style smackdown. Many of my friends back in those days got beatings too from one or both parents. It was kind of normal.

But there was also a semi-nurturing side to my dad. My father rarely went anywhere with us. He expressed his love by teaching me how to work on cars and fix things around the house. While I appreciate the instruction and tools he gave me, I can't say I ever looked up to him as a role model. I have mixed emotions about him. Nothing about my life should have turned out right, but I am surprisingly well-adjusted and successful. There were many great things about my childhood and those are the memories that I choose to hold on to. For all of us the past is fuzzy and compartmentalized. We have rooms and rooms of memories that we can access. I have chosen to keep a few doors closed that don't help me move forward. I know those negative, traumatic memory rooms are there. I just try not to spend unnecessary time in them.

My brother Jon and I talk from time to time about our childhood. He probably acted out a bit more in reaction to my father's abuse than I did. I am 10 years younger than he is and 22 years younger than Brian. Maybe our father was tired of beating on us by the time I came around because Brian and Jon probably got the worst of it. Whatever the case, Jon and I made it. Brian did not. Brian turned to the bottle to ease the pain of his existence and that decision to drink cost him his life. He could not overcome the abuse of my father and the fact that his biological mother abandoned him—even though my mother took him in at the age of two and loved him like her own.

As a teen, Jon told me he wanted to kill our father. That was how deep he felt the pain. I'm glad he did not do it. I asked why he didn't. "I knew I couldn't get away with it in God's eyes," was his reply. His faith in God and understanding heaven and hell saved his life and my father's life. In the end Jon felt that his love of God was more powerful than his hatred of our father. Jon went on to have a successful career in the Air Force before becoming a pastor and hospice chaplain. Our faith helped both of us find our purpose. Instead of holding on to the hurt and negativity of our past, we decided to share some of our experiences and help others find their paths in life. As a hospice chaplain, my brother helps people and their families transition through the pain and emotion of death. It is amazing the reflection that takes place in that context. Those that have found their calling and who have lived an ideal life understand who they are and leave this life with few regrets.

I have no ill will toward my father. What purpose would it serve for me to hate a dead man? What purpose would it serve for me to hold anger towards an uneducated country boy who probably disciplined us the way he had been disciplined? My father was born in 1907 in Kosciusko, Mississippi. He had only an eighth grade education. He was 21 years older than my mother. She was his fourth wife. Remember, culture and context always matter. At the time the Deep South was not a warm and friendly place for Negroes, as they were called then. Maybe I am making an excuse for his past, but it's clear to me my father was shaped and honed in a time when he was less than. He was not colored, black, or African-American. He was a cotton-picking Negro from Mississippi. So I forgive him, and I am thankful for the good parts of our 14 years together.

*At the end of each day I can say, I made it. At the beginning of each morning I can say, I have another chance to improve myself or the circumstances that are before me.* Whether I am 100 percent at fault for the challenges in my life or not, I can do things to change the situation, even if it means forgiving myself. Forgiving ourselves can be hardest of all. It is often easier to forgive someone else than to forgive ourselves. Here are a few steps that can help you begin to let go of the past.

## Exercise 4: Steps for Letting Go

1. **Understand that your past memories may actually betray you.** We think that memories are stored in our brains like data on a computer hard drive. We think that we can recall the information in its original form and that over time the facts don't change. We convince ourselves we know exactly how events in our lives unfolded.

   Neuroscientists have shown that each time we remember something, we reconstruct the event, reassembling it from bits and pieces of data throughout the brain. "Psychologists have pointed out that we also suppress memories that are painful or damaging to self-esteem. We could say that, as a result, memory is unreliable. We could also say it is adaptive, reshaping itself to accommodate the new situations we find ourselves facing."[51] Either way, we have to face the fact that memory is flexible and dynamic.

   Most of us recall a rosier past than we actually had. Some of us are tormented by painful memories we can't shake and that seem to get worse every time we revisit them. But all of us carry incomplete portraits of our pasts.

2. **Understand that you can't undo the past.** Life does not have an eraser. You can shape only your future. No matter how much anger you carry or how many regrets you have, you cannot undo what was.

My fifth grade teacher shared this lesson with me and my friends. He would remind us anytime we tried to argue our point or throw a tantrum when conflict happened on the playground. Mr. Knox would say, "Flush it, it is over, let it die." He was quick to tell us to move on. The past is gone and deserves as much attention as the waste we leave behind. When I was a cadet leader at the Air Force Academy, I gave one bad command during a drill competition that caused my group to come in second. Folks were mad at me, but I could not change the outcome. I moved on. Yes, I remember it, but that one mistake doesn't define me.

3. **Understand that time can heal old wounds.** Think of a wound in your flesh. Though painful at first, the wound will heal with proper care and treatment. We will be left with a scar, but over time the scar itself fades and we hardly notice it. Each of the scars on my body has a story, but the older I get, the harder it is for me to remember what caused them. A few scars are more prominent than others, typically those are the ones I picked at or did not allow to heal properly.

I believe our memories were designed the way they are so that we can cope and move on with life.

Imagine what would happen if football players or tennis players quit every time they made a mistake—Serena Williams would collapse every time she had an unforced error in a match or Tom Brady would get into his car and drive away every time he threw an interception. Even in business you have to recover from mistakes. I made decisions that cost tens of thousands of dollars. We all make mistakes, but those mistakes can't be our anchor. We can't constantly go back and revisit the pains in our past if we hope to heal. You can't pick at the scab. Time is the great healer.

4. **Decide to move forward.** We can decide to move forward and release the anchor of our past. There is an old saying credited to banker J.P. Morgan, "The first step towards getting somewhere is to decide that you are not going to stay where you are." I often see addicts, including some of my own family members who were never successful in their recovery because they kept the same circle of friends. They kept going to places that reminded them of their addiction. While we may not be addicted to drugs, some of us are addicted to the drama of life. Peace and well-being are destinations we must choose. If we want to live the IDEAL life, we must move in a direction that takes us there. Sometimes that means leaving behind the source of our suffering and other distractions.

5. **Take responsibility for your suffering.** Too often we blame others or our circumstances for our fear and failure. When people come to me for counseling about relationships, I always let them know that they are at least 50 percent of the problem. We are the sum total of our choices. We

choose how we react to situations that we are in. We sometimes choose to stay in abusive relationships and situations because we are afraid to leave. We often fear the unknown, so we stay in the unhealthy present. Sometimes life just happens; we may be involved in an accident or a natural disaster. Some situations are definitely out of our control. But we control our fight, our heart, our reaction. We can run and hide, or we can take the responsibility to get the help that we need. Yes, part of taking responsibility is acknowledging that we need help.

Many government programs, community organizations, and kind individuals can offer you help. You have to be brave enough to ask for it. When you have been traumatized, you may feel as though you don't have any control over your life. Family, friends, and others will try to tell you what to do. You can follow their advice, but be aware that you are choosing to do so. If you are a minor, it is important that you make decisions with people you trust. And, ultimately, you are responsible for your own behavior. Being traumatized is not an acceptable excuse for behavior that hurts you or hurts others.

6. **Develop new stories.** I was determined to be a better man than my father. I still have some anger and insecurity inside of me that developed at an early age. Yet, I resist those urges every day because I want to create my own story. I want my son and daughter to respect me—not out of fear, but because they love me. They won't remember any head slaps because that's not the way I discipline them. They won't remember any profanity-laced tirades. I am an integral part of my children's lives. Even though they are college age, they still call me for advice and guidance. They still enjoy coming home and doing things with dad.

You have the power to overcome your negative past. Don't be what you fear. Be your own champion and choose a path the makes you proud of yourself. Sure there will be ups and downs and failure along the way, but as long as your heart beats and breath oozes from your lungs, your story is still being written.

7. **Know that it is okay to let go.** "Holding on is believing that there's only a past; letting go is knowing that there's a future," writes author Daphne Rose Kingma.[51] Once the lessons of the past have been learned, we need to give ourselves permission to release the past. Have you ever started down the road in your car? Do you keep going in the wrong direction and say, "Well, I spent so much time driving north I can turn east now?" That would be a pretty dumb decision, wouldn't it? You would never wind up at your preferred destination. Would you stay on a plane headed to Russia when you were supposed to go to Hawaii? No, you wouldn't; you would correct the error at the first opportunity you had.

Often in life we feel stuck. We say, "I've invested too much time and effort in this to change. I can't leave friends; they will be hurt." We even take on the pain of others who share similar experiences. What starts as a support group becomes an anchor of despair. Instead of getting the support we need to heal our wounds, we become stagnant with people who guilt us into not moving forward.

Many people struggle with the concept of moving forward. Let's think about it in religious terms. Then, it's very simple. Repent. I don't mean confessing your sins or begging for forgiveness as some traditionally interpret the word. The Greek word for *repent* is μετάνοια (metanoia). It literally means to change your mind. Letting go of the past and moving forward often means changing your mind— changing your mind as to how you think about the past, how you react to the past, how you feel about the future, and about what you will do in the future.

8. **Develop healthy relationships.** A biblical proverb says, "As iron sharpens iron, so a friend sharpens a friend" (Proverbs 27:17 NLT). Not many of us can go it alone in life. We need people to walk with us as we journey along our chosen paths. Who we surround ourselves with says a great deal about who we are and where we are going in life. My former pastor often said to me, "If you want to know who you are, look at your friends. If you want to know where you are going, look at your leaders." The lesson stuck with me. To be successful, we have to surround ourselves with the right team and stay away from those who don't share our same vision and values.

9. **Stand tall and acknowledge your pain.** The lessons of our past pain can give us wisdom and insight, enabling us to walk a better path.

On my right bicep I have a burn scar that has almost faded beyond perception, but from time to time, I look at it and remember the story of how I got it. I couldn't have been more than 12 or 13 years of age when I decided to do an experiment in our garage. I got some matches, some Black Cat firecrackers, and a can of gasoline. I am sure you are thinking, "What could possibly go wrong, Glen?" Somehow curiosity caused me to combine these elements on top of a 45-pound metal plate weight and light them on fire in our garage. BOOM! Gasoline and fire exploded all over the garage. I put the fire out just as quickly as it ignited and ran into the house to answer a phone call from a friend. As I joked with my friend about my unwise teenage experiment, something caught my attention. Out of the corner of my eye I saw the black tar paper lining our garage wall suddenly engulfed in flames. I dismissed my friend, hung up the phone on the kitchen wall, and ran outside to tackle the flames. I grabbed a blanket and beat the flames into submission. My heart pounded. Sweat ran down my quivering body. It was the middle of summer in Houston,

Texas. The flames only intensified the heat and humidity that are native to the summertime in the Bayou City. I sat there thankful—thankful I did not burn down my house and thankful that my parents were not home (because I was certain at the time that my dad would have killed me). I felt numb, but then the pain slowly drove its way to the surface. I look down at my inner bicep and noticed blisters beginning to form. Somehow, someway I had been touched by the fire.

Other than a melted weight bench cover, the scar on my arm would be my only reminder of a tragedy averted. It remains visible wisdom, a permanent whisper to make better choices. But the pain was also acknowledgement that I was alive. Ultimately the cost of my gasoline experiment could have been a lot higher, so maybe it was a sign that I was also kissed by the grace of God. When you stand tall, you embrace your scars and you use them to help yourself and others move forward and avoid future pain.

10. **Create a new definition of you.** "Never look back unless you are planning to go that way" is a saying often attributed to Henry David Thoreau. Create a new definition of yourself; write your own story. People will try to bring up your past, but you'll need to continue to construct your own narrative. If this means shutting down your social media accounts, do it. If it means changing your cell number, do it. If it means moving to find better opportunities, do it. Just have a plan.

    I am not talking about running away from responsibility; I am talking about running towards a better you. Sometimes our pride holds us back and sometimes creating a new definition means acknowledging that our old story is the wrong story. If you are drowning in debt, maybe you need to get credit counseling (while developing better habits) or cut up your credit cards. If you are struggling academically, maybe you need to change majors or schools. If you cannot take care of a child, maybe you need to consider adoption (a hard choice but sometimes choices like this are necessary). If a child can be placed with a loving family member or a loving stranger, why wouldn't we choose that option over abortion or poverty?

    Creating a new you requires careful planning and wise counsel. The examples I used above all have certain societal stigmas attached to them. People will say that if you change schools, file for bankruptcy, or put up a child for adoption, you are a quitter. But they are all perfectly legal and solid methods to overcome past mistakes and poor choices that have been used by successful people to help them continue to move forward in life.

**Glen's Guidance**

- We have to let go of the past to move toward our ideal future.
- Be relevant in the present.
- If you allow it to, the past can hold you prisoner.
- Don't mix firecrackers and gasoline!

NOTES

# Chapter 11

# Supportive Community

*"Alone we can do so little; together we can do so much."*
—Helen Keller[53]

Developing a healthy identity means surrounding yourself with healthy supporters. I believe in the power of the community. It keeps us from becoming narcissistic and focusing only on ourselves. Nothing good comes from navel gazing and picking out our flaws. It is much better to assemble your own Dream Team. The four types of people we need in our supportive community are: encouragers, grounders, pullers, and pushers.

**Encouragers.** Encouragers are our cheerleaders. If we had our preference, many of us would start our teams with encouragers and there is nothing wrong with that. But you have to have the right balance of these people on your team. Let's face it: life can be hard. Even when you live your IDEAL, life is not always easy. We experience stress, brokenness, and pain. There are times when we find ourselves right on the edge, ready to give up on our dreams and on ourselves. We might get to the point where we feel like we can't take it anymore. When this happens, sometimes the only difference between going on or giving up—succeeding or failing—is a simple word of encouragement. We need people on our team who will inspire us and help us to move forward. The encourager has no problem giving us aid, support, and help.

Encouragers come in many forms. They can be friends, family or even coworkers. Their positivity helps to keep us motivated. Their faith in us fans our passion and our belief in ourselves.

**Grounders.** Grounders help us keep things in perspective as we plan and execute our vision. Grounders tell it like it is and keep us from getting big heads. They can keep us on track and will often challenge our dreams. Grounders do not avoid conflicts and criticism. They have a keen eye for the errors and shortcomings of others and are often quick at expressing criticism.

Grounders will sometimes rub you the wrong way, especially when they do not readily accept your ideas or dreams. A grounder will ask tough questions based on facts. They will sometimes tear apart your ideas like a forensic medical examiner investigating a crime scene. But the right grounder will always speak the truth in love.

**Pullers.** Pullers have been there before. They are your mentors and goal models, people who have a proven record of success. They can help to blaze the trail for you. They can pull you to greater heights because they have the skills, position, or connections. As we think about where we want to go on our journey, we appreciate having people around us who have obtained the level of success that we desire. Talking to someone who has "been there and done that" helps us to keep our vision in perspective. The right puller will always help us overcome the challenges that we are facing.

**Pushers.** Finally the pushers are those people who are coming up behind us. They look up to us; they sometimes want to be us and we wonder why. While I am a strong advocate of intrinsic motivation to help us live our IDEAL life, sometimes being a mentor to someone else can be all the motivation that we need to move forward with our own lives. The pusher stands behind you every step of the way. Sometimes when you are afraid to move forward or take that leap of faith, the perfect pusher will be there to give you a gentle nudge.

It's like running a race or running on the treadmill in the gym. It seems like I can always go a little faster when someone is creeping up behind me or I can eyeball the pace of the person on the treadmill next to me. Everyone does not thrive on friendly competition, but it sure helps me. We all need a little push from time to time. Seeing that others can do it often unlocks that little bit of extra in our own mind. Knowing that someone is right on our heels can help us pick up the pace if we are feeling down.

I like John Donne's famous poem from 1623 which, if he were writing it today, would say this: "No one is an island, entire of itself. Everyone is a piece of the continent, part of the main." Not many of us can successfully live this life alone. I don't believe it is healthy and I question why our Creator would design us for oblivion. I doubt that God would.

Rather, we are designed to live in community. We are designed to fit uniquely into this puzzling life of pieces in a jigsaw puzzle. I remember my daughter took months to put together one of those 1,000 piece puzzles. It was a black and white photo of the Brooklyn Bridge in New York City. She got down to the 998th piece and numbers 999 and 1000 were missing. We tore the house apart looking for those pieces. Why? Even though the puzzle was 99.8 percent complete, it seemed worthless without the final two pieces. We eventually found the pieces and now the puzzle is proudly on display on the wall of her college apartment. We are best in the midst of others.

You are just as important to someone as those pieces were to that puzzle. Without you the world's picture is incomplete.

## Glen's Guidance

- This life is not meant to go it alone.
- Get the support you need.
- You are an important piece of the puzzle.

# NOTES

_____

_____

_____

_____

_____

_____

_____

_____

_____

# Conclusion

# Enjoy the Journey

*"Happiness is a direction, not a place."*
*—Sydney J. Harris*[54]

The journey is the most important part of finding your purpose. The path we take in life is much more important than the destination.

I often take trips with my family and I do about 90 percent of the driving while the rest of the family is out cold. Our family road trips go something like this. Everyone piles into the car. We all plug in our devices. The kids sit in the back listening to their playlists. I turn on ESPN radio or some other talk station, set the Waze app, and we start on our journey. Typically our road trips are four and a half hours or less—more than that and my wife and my daughter cast me aside for Delta Airlines. On our short trips, my wife and I talk about 30 minutes before she gets bored from listening to my road trip stories which she has heard a thousand times. Her mouth falls open and her head tips back—her sign for: "I'm out, buddy; you're on your own." Then it is just me and the radio until we hit our destination.

I don't mind long road trips. I find them quite relaxing and peaceful. To me, the experience of the open road is far better than being closed up in a plane. When I was a kid, we often took road trips as a family. A couple of times each year my family would pile into our 1973 Buick Apollo and drive 506 miles from Houston, Texas, to Kosciusko, Mississippi, to visit my grandparents. We did not have GPS; we had the *Rand McNally Road Atlas*. That atlas didn't just list directions, but it showed places of interests, topographical features, and historical landmarks. I remember tracing each and every mile of the journey with my finger. I loved flipping back and forth and preparing for the exact moment that I crossed a state line—oh, how I wanted there to be a real line on the highway. Following the road atlas meant paying attention to the road signs and the scenery. I was tuned into every mile of that 506-mile journey. Now with GPS I am pretty much on autopilot. I don't pay attention in the same way. I just point the car and wait for the Australian woman in the little box to tell me what to do.

As we journey along life's road, we often find ourselves on autopilot. We set the cruise control and coast through life. We wake up, go to work or school, come home, eat dinner, go to bed, and start the same cycle all over again. Somewhere along our life's journey we have put our heads down and missed the blessings that God has placed before us. We need to hit the brakes, lift our heads, and enjoy the journey.

The path we take in life shapes and molds us. It prepares us for the final destination. If we take the easy road and cut corners, we will be ill-prepared when we arrive at our destination. If we take the hard road, we can wind up at our destination bitter and burnt out. But if we take our time, go through the process, and appreciate each and every mile along the journey, we arrive at our destination refreshed and prepared for the challenges that we will experience there.

# The IDEAL is a JOURNEY,
## not a destination.

The tools in this guidebook are somewhat like the apps many of you have on your phones or like that old road atlas I used to have as a child. My Waze app alerts me to speed traps, accidents, traffic jams, and other hazards and helps me pick the most expedient path to my destination based on the options I choose. I could just input the destination, follow that voice, and get to where I need to be, but there is so much more to life and my road trip than just getting there.

As I drive, I see people and animals beside the road. I see dead animals littering various highways. Sometimes I see accidents and wonder how in the world did that happen? Strange cars and unknown people pass me by, and I think to myself, "Where are they going and what are they doing to entertain themselves?"

Then I see the famous Texas gas station Buc-ee's and its big beaver logo, and I stop. On every single road trip, I stop at Buc-ee's. Buc-ee's is like a truck stop on steroids, Texas-style. The one in New Braunfels is the largest convenience store in the world so I'm not exaggerating when I say if the zombie apocalypse happened and you were at Buc-ee's, you would survive. They have hot food, desserts, drinks, humongous and very clean restrooms, clothes, tacos, beef jerky, BBQ sandwiches, BBQ pits, Texas flags, Texas kolaches, pickled eggs, YETI coolers, and, best of all, those caramel and butter-glazed corn puffs called Beaver Nuggets. Yum! You can spend literally thousands of hours and thousands of dollars in Buc-ee's. Now Buc-ee's is not my end destination, but it is a wonderful part of every drive that I look forward to.

As we set off on our journey to "Becoming Me," we have to stop and smell the roses. *There are so many interesting and exciting adventures on our path to living the IDEAL life, and we should take the opportunity to experience them.* On our road trips I often feel that my family misses so many things as they sleep. We all arrive at the same destination at the same time, but I get the privilege of experiencing all the great views and interesting places that are part of our journey.

Sure thing, distractions will take us off the path we are called to, but that does not mean we can't enjoy the blessing and privileges that are on the journey. Since we were little children we probably cried, "Are we there yet?" I get that question from my family and I am sure I asked my parents that when we took our nine-hour road trips to Kosciusko, Mississippi. But as I reflect, in some ways the preparation and travel were just as impactful to who I am not as a person than what actually happened once I arrived at my grandmother's home.

Living life with the question "Who Am I?" is like living with deferred dreams. We live, but we don't thrive. Instead of each day being life-giving, each day becomes a burden. If we are not careful, we can explode under the pressure. We all have something to contribute to this world. Accept yourself and your gifts. As you discover your call and live your IDEAL, you will live your life with confidence, no matter what your role.

Some of us are out front, some of us are in the middle, and some of us pull up the rear, but that does not make any of us less significant. We need each other. Pastors can be fantastic preachers, but they need congregations to speak to every Sunday morning. Without the people in the pews, they are just persons in empty buildings. Famed soccer player Cristiano Renaldo is a world class forward, but he would not be successful without other players to pass him the ball and the goalie to defend his team's goal. The model in front of the lens requires the photographer behind the camera to create the perfect photograph.

I hope this book has been helpful for you. Writing it has truly been a blessing and a journey for me. It has allowed me to reflect back on my life, where I have been and where I want to go. Writing is a labor of love that for me is setting a direction for the next phase of who I want to be. There is a certain peace that overcomes you when you get comfortable in your own skin, when you start to experience that IDEAL life.

I wrote part of this book over a Christmas holiday (okay, if I am honest, a couple of Christmas holidays, but this last story refers to the last holiday right before I completed the book). I was able to spend time with my brother Jon, his family, and our 89-year old mother. We are 10 years apart but there is no doubt that Jon and I are brothers—although it must be said that I am the taller, better-looking sibling. It is scary sometimes to see and listen to your family. It is easy to see the bad habits, the mannerisms, and other odd patterns that come from being raised in the same home.

My wife and kids have no problem pointing these things out on the three-hour drive home from Houston to San Antonio. Sure everyone sleeps unless it's "let's talk about daddy time." Then everyone is awake and engaged. My daughter even remarked how much my brother and I sound alike. Clearly our home environment has shaped many aspects of who Jon and I are. We are similar in many ways, some good and some, well, not so good. But we are also very different. We made different choices, we made different decisions, which means although we are brothers, we are also individuals. Every time I go home for the holidays I am reminded how much we are shaped by our environment. I am also reminded that we can overcome that environment. I am reminded of things that I have let go. I am also reminded of a few things that I have hung on to. Holiday homecomings can become in-your-face, I AM and I DECIDE moments. I love the family that I was given, but I am also thankful for the choices I have been able to make moving forward.

Keep this book handy and reflect on the various exercises from time to time if you are ever feeling lost or overwhelmed as you journey through life. It can help you refocus. At the very least, stand in front of a mirror and say to yourself.

I AM…the sum total of my choices, my experiences, and my environment.

I DECIDE…the path I will follow and how I will respond to life.

I EVOLVE…to stay relevant in a dynamic and sometimes unpredictable world.

I ADVANCE…by honing my skills and being the best I can be.

I LET GO…of past hurts, failures, and negative experiences in order to move forward.

I don't know your dreams. I don't know your IDEAL path, but I encourage you to begin your journey today with the same passion as the monk who heard the song.

Let me remind you one last time:

> I want you to *live your life*, and I want you to *love the life you live*.

I look forward to hearing from you as you share all the great things that are happening with you as you decide to reach for your IDEAL life. I am envisioning a whole new cadre of young people emailing me and writing me their stories of letting go and moving on. Many of you will become my pushers and encouragers as you apply what you read in this book. Picking up this book and getting to the end of it is just one step, but I know that you have a great and productive journey ahead of you.

# Live your LIFE.
# Love the life you LIVE.

# NOTES

# Helpful Resources

Here is a list of resources that may help you as you seek to live YOUR IDEAL life.

**Official website for IDEAL Me:** www.IDEALmeBook.com. Check out this website for updates and more resources related to this book and to get updates from the author.

**Author's website:** www.GlenGuyton.com. Reach out to the author, follow his blog, or request information for speaking engagements.

**National Domestic Abuse Hotline:** Phone and chat services are available to anyone who has been affected by relationship abuse, including those who are currently in abusive relationships, those who are working to heal, friends or family of victims and survivors and anyone in the community who has questions about domestic violence. The hotline can provide phone services in more than 200 languages. www.thehotline.org  1-800-799-7233 1-800-787-3224 (TTY for deaf/hard of hearing)

**National Runaway Safeline:** You can expect to share your story with someone who won't judge or tell you what to do. Each team member has been trained to handle a crisis, provide support, and listen to your story. See www.1800runaway.org/youth-teens/, call 1-800-RUNAWAY, or text 66008.

**National Suicide Prevention Lifeline:** This national network of local crisis centers provides free and confidential emotional support to people in suicidal crisis or emotional distress 24 hours a day, 7 days a week. See online at suicidepreventionlifeline.org or call 1-800-273-8255 (1-800-799-4889 for the deaf and hard of hearing).

# Notes

1. James Patterson (novel) and Marc Moss (screenplay), *Along Came a Spider*, DVD, directed by Lee Tamahori, Los Angeles: Paramount Pictures, 2001.

2. Used with permission from Carnisha Carroll.

3. Jacob and Wilhelm Grimm, et. al, "Snow White and the Seven Dwarfs," movie, Walt Disney Productions, 1937.

4. Patrick Nelson, "The Heaviest Smartphone Users Click, Tap or Swipe on Their Phones 5,427 Times a Day," *Network World*, July 7, 2016, https://www.networkworld.com/article/3092446/smartphones/we-touch-our-phones-2617-times-a-day-says-study.html.

5. Maggie Fox, "Half of All Teenagers Are Addicted to Their Smartphones, Survey Finds," *NBC News*, May 3, 2016.

6. Karol Markowicz, "America's ugly epidemic of social media envy," New York Post, January 16, 2014, https://nypost.com/2014/01/16/americas-ugly-epidemic-of-social-media-envy

7. Daniel J. DeNoon, "Early Retirement, Early Death?," *Web MD*, October 20, 1005, http://www.webmd.com/healthy-aging/news/20051020/early-retirement-early-death.

8. Natasha Tracy, "Why Do Teens Commit Suicide? Causes of Teen Suicide," *Healthy Place for Your Mental Health*, last modified June 17, 2016, http://www.healthyplace.com/suicide/why-do-teens-commit-suicide-causes-of-teen-suicide.

9. Siedah Garrett and Glen Ballard, "Man in the Mirror," performed by Michael Jackson, et. al., recorded 1988, Epic, compact disc single.

10. Olii Kiviruusu, Noora Berg, Taina Huurre, Hillevi Aro, Mauri Martunen, and Ari Haukkala, "Interpersonal Conflicts and Development of Self-Esteem from Adolescence to Mid-Adulthood. A 26-Year Follow-Up." Abstract. *PlosONE*, (October 18, 2016), doi:10.1371/journal.pone.0164941.

11. Miraca U.M. Gross, "The 'Me' Behind the Mask: Intellectually Gifted Students and the Search for Identity," *Roeper Review* 20, No. 3, (1998), 167.

12. Julie Ricevuto, "Why It's Awesome Coco Rocha Is Spilling the Beans on the 'No Makeup' Look," (blog), posted July 1, 2016, https//www.yahoo.com/beauty/why-its-awesome-coco-rocha-is-spilling-the-beans-172732819.html.

13. Tina Williamson, "5 Masks We Wear and Why We Should Take Them Off," HUFFPOST (blog), updated July 13, 2016, https://www.huffingtonpost.com/tina-williamson/5-masks-we-wear-and-why-w_b_7786922.html.

14. Glen A. Larson, "Song from 'Buck Rogers' (Suspension)," performed by Kipp Lennon, recorded 1979, MCA Records MCA-41026, 45 rpm.

15. Salvador Dali, AZ Quotes.com, Wind and Fly LTD, 2017, http://www.azquotes.com/author/3592-Salvador_Dali, accessed November 17, 2017.

16. Kari Hartel, "Exercise and Healthy Eating vs Genetics: What Really Determines Body Shape?," *FitDay*, accessed January 13, 2018, https://www.fitday.com/fitness-articles/fitness/exercise-healthy-eating-vs-genetics-which-really-determines-body-shape.html.

17. "Weight Loss Market to Reach $672 Billion by 2015," Marketwired, September 27, 2011, http://www.marketwired.com/press-release/weight-loss-market-to-reachbillion-by-2015-1565973.htm.

18. "The 10 Shortest Players in NBA History," Sports Management Degree Hub, June 26, 2013, https://www.sportsmanagementdegreehub.com/the-10-shortest-players-in-nba-history/.

19. "Hoarding Fact Sheet," International OCD Foundation, (2009), https://iocdf.org/wp-content-uploads/2014/10/Hoarding-Fact-Sheet.pdf.

20. Adapted from Southern Cross University Career Center.

21. Del Hershberger, "Vocation and Occupation: How to Respond to God's Call on Your Life," *Mennonite Mission Network*, November 22, 2016, https://www.mennonitemission.net/blog/Vocation-and-occupation-How-to-respond-to-God%E2%80%99s-call-on-your.life.

22. "Bill Gates Biography," *The Biography.com Website*, A&E Television Networks, updated November 13, 2017, http://www.biography.com/people/bill-gates-9307520.

23. Anna Vital, "How Bill Gates Started—Infographic," *Adioma*, (blog), accessed September 21, 2016, http://fundersandfounders.com/how-bill-gates-started/.

24. "Curtis Martin Enshrinement Speech," Pro Football Hall of Fame, August 4, 2012, http://www.profootballhof.com/players/curtis-martin/enshrinement/.

25. Tejvan Pettinger, "Biography J.K. Rowling," *Biography Online*, Oxford, U.K., updated November 6, 2017, http://www.biographyonline.net/writers/j_k_rowling.html.

26. Emma-Victoria Farr, "J.K. Rowling: 10 Facts about the Writer," *The Telegraph*, Telegraph Media Group, September 27, 2012, www.telegraph.co.uk/culture/books/booknews/9564894/JK-Rowling-10-facts-about-the-writer.html.

27. "President John F. Kennedy's Address at Rice University on the Nation's Space Effort, September 12, 1962," *National Aeronautics and Space Administration*, https://er.jsc.nasa.gov/seh/ricetalk.htm.

28. Ibid.

29. "Quote by Martin Luther King Jr.," *Quotery*, accessed June 29, 2017, http://www.quotery.com/quotes/even-if-it-falls-your-lot-to-be-a-street/.

30. "Waste Management, Inc. (WM)," *New York Stock Exchange*, accessed January 12, 2018, https://finance.yahoo.com/q/ks?s=WM.

31. Chris Morton, "Vocation: Five Tips for Discovering What to Do with Your Life." *Missio Alliance*, September 22, 2016, http://www.missioalliance.org/vocation-five-tips-discovering-live/.

32. Shannon Skinner, *The Whispering Heart: Your Inner Guide to Creativity*, in "The Price You Must Pay to Follow Your Dreams," (blog) HUFFPOST, last modified September 11, 2012, http://www.huffingtonpost.ca/shannon-skinner/the-price-of-success_b_1666909.html.

33. Graham Hayes, "New Role, Same Competitive Drive," ESPNW, December 13, 2012, http://jstilesonline.com/about/news-articles/news-articles-2012/1359-2/.

34. Rachael Rettner, "Chris Borland Leaves NFL: The Science of Football and Brain Injury," *Live Science*, March 17, 2015, http://www.livescience.com/50163-football-cte-brain-disease-risk.html.

35. Shaunacy Ferro, "Scientists Debunk the Myth That 10,000 Hours of Practice Makes You An Expert," CO.DESIGN, March 12, 2014, http://www.fastcodesign.com/3027564/asides/scientists-debunk-the-myth that-10000-hours-of-practice-makes-you-an-expert.

36. "Defining Countable Athletically Related Activities," NCAA, accessed January 11, 2018,   http://www.ncaa.org/sites/default/files/Charts.pdf.

37. Madeline Jones, "Plus Size Bodies, What Is Wrong with Them Anyway?" *Plus Model Magazine*, January 8, 2012, http://plus-model-mag.com/2012/01/plus-size-bodies-what-is-wrong-with-them-anyway/.

38. Jonathan Larson, "Seasons of Love," *Rent*, album, 1996.

39. "Ernest Hemingway Quotes," BrainyQuote.com, Xplore Inc., accessed January 15, https://www.brainyquote.com/quotes/ernest_hemingway_174758.

40. *English Oxford Living Dictionaries*, s.v. "life," accessed January 11, 2018, https://en.oxforddictionaries.com/definition/life.

41. *Merriam-Webster*, s.v. "evolution," accessed January 11, 2018, https://www.merriam-webster.com/dictionary/evolution.

42. "Al Bundy," *Married with Children Wiki*, accessed January 11, 2018, http://marriedwithchildren.wikia.com/wiki/Al_Bundy.

43. "Largest Industries by State, 1990-2013" from the Bureau of Labor Statistics, U.S. Department of Labor, *The Economics Daily*, accessed January 11, 2018, http://www.bls.gov/opub/ted/2014/ted_20140728.htm.

44. "Hakeem Olajuwon Biography.com," *The Biography.com website*, A&E Television Networks, last modified February 4, 2016, http://www.biography.com/people/hakeem-olajuwon-21101363#synopsis.

45. "Barack Obama's Feb. 5 Speech," *The New York Times*, February 5, 2008, http://www.nytimes.com/2008/02/05/us/politics/05text-obama.html.

46. Langston Hughes, "Harlem," *The Collected Poems* of Langston Hughes, (New York: Vintage Books, 1994).

47. D'Vera Cohn and Rich Morin, "American Mobility: Who Moves? Who Stays Put? Where's Home?" Pew Research Center, last modified December 29, 2008, http://assets.pewresearch.org/wp-content/uploads/sites/3/2011/04/American-Mobility-Report-updated-12-29-08.pdf.

48. Bear Grylls, *A Survival Guide for Life: How to Achieve Your Goals, Thrive in Adversity and Grow in Character*. (London: Corgi Books, 2016).

49. "Henry David Thoreau Quotes," BrainyQuote.com, Xplore Inc., accessed January 15, 2018, https://www.brainyquote.com/quotes/henry_david_thoreau_382352.

50. Used with permission from Crystal Washington.

51. Ken Eisold, "Unreliable Memory," *Psychology Today*, accessed January 11, 2018, https://www.psychologytoday.com/blog/hidden-motives/201203/unreliable-memory.

52. Stephanie A. Sarkis, "Quotes on Letting Go," *Psychology Today*, October 25, 2012,  https://www.psychologytoday.com/blog/here-there-and-everywhere/201210/quotes-letting-go.

53. "Helen Keller Quotes," BrainyQuote.com, Xplore Inc., accessed January 15, 2018, https://www.brainyquote.com/quotes/helen_keller_382259,.

54. "Sydney J. Harris Quotes," BrainyQuote.com, Xplore Inc, 2018, accessed January 15, 2018, https://www.brainyquote.com/quotes/sydney_j_harris_105550.

# Author's Page

Glen Guyton works with individuals trying to make sense of the culture in which they live so that they can live their IDEAL lives—the subject of this book. Be encouraged to live your life and love the life you live.

Glen's expertise in understanding culture has taken him from being a nerdy kid growing up in the Houston suburbs to becoming an Air Force officer and teaching middle school to serving as the executive director of a national nonprofit faith organization.

Cultural competence means understanding how various generations engage the world. He is also passionate about giving back to the community and helping young people develop the skills they need to not only survive, but to thrive in a dynamic world. His StepOut! Podcast helps youth and young adults—and also those who love them—to define for themselves what success means.

Glen holds a Bachelor of Science Degree in Management from the United States Air Force Academy and a Master of Education Degree from Regent University.

CPSIA information can be obtained
at www.ICGtesting.com
Printed in the USA
LVHW032013150321
681602LV00003B/816